Published in Nottingham by Thin Blue Line Books

ISBN 978-1-3999-3182-3

THE SHARP END

Murder, Violence and Knife Crime on Nottingham's Thin Blue Line

This book is dedicated to the following colleagues who have been a real influence on me throughout my career, become genuine friends or supported me in other ways. In no particular order:

Rob and Tindall – The 'November Team'; Gav, McQueef, Geordie Lee, Will, Little LeeLee, Justice John and Paul – What a team we made; James 'The Batman', Vicky P and Nicola – thank you for your patience and imparting your knowledge to me; Wildey, 'Raddy Steve', 'Cartel', 'Aussie' and 'Londoner' for teaching me the value of pro-active policing; 'The General' – a true friend and confidante, as well as expert 'proof-reader'; Special Emma and Will – for making volunteering fun; "Can you just" Geoffrey and Lorna, Bonner and Mark – thanks for mostly being kind to me…; "Who the hell is" Dan, Spuds, Forest and De'barge – Tactical Traffic Squad; All the officers from the Mighty 2 Section Central, 2 Section 'Radford Circus', Canning-on-the-hill and the Great 3 Section Radford Road; Jessy C, Retsof, Matt, Mike, Tractor James and Abi 2 – all those free hours you worked with me; And anyone else who I've had the amazing pleasure to work with over the years.

You've all made an impact on me in some small way, and you all do an amazing job.

I would also like to take the time to thank my parents, without whom I would not have had this amazing career to date; as well as my in-laws who have provided childcare and support over the last half a decade or more.

Final and most important thanks go to my children whose constant love, affection and comedy moments provide me the inspiration to keep going, and especially to my wife, who took much more than her fair share of childcare during my time as a police officer and never moaned about it.

The Sharp End

Chapters

Introduction

Being a Police Officer was all I can ever remember wanting to do. Unlike many children, my desired career choice never changed. I was taken in at a young age by my neighbour James French, who was a traffic officer with Wiltshire Police, who regularly turned up at my parents' house as a tea stop in his Rover police car.

On one occasion he came to visit at a time when my mum had her hands full with a two-year old me and my six-month old twin brothers, all needing her attention. Rather than assessing the situation and thinking he might come back another day, PC French still wanted some liquid refreshment. A hurried "help yourself, you know where everything is" from Mrs Andrews, and James was soon enjoying a warm beverage. A minute or two later, my ever on-the-ball mum had a breather and asked him "which milk did you use?" Breastfeeding two always-hungry twins meant that she had to store her milk, and what better to keep it in than milk bottles? "The one in the fridge", was the puzzled answer from the uniformed officer. "That fridge?" "yeah, that one". "Oh. That's *my* milk James." "Yes, you said to help myself". "No", paused my Mum, "that's *My. Milk*". As the penny dropped with the visiting guest, the tea cup was lowered slowly to the table, and his face grew greener and greener. It wasn't long before my mum was unable to hold her laughter in anymore and the young Traffic Cop realised the joke that had been played on him.

This was just one of the many stories from PC French that became mini legends in my household. Others included telling some American tourists at Stonehenge who asked "Gee, is it really that old?", that in fact it wasn't. The original stones were too valuable to leave out in the elements, and were now in storage in the British

Museum basement. The ones the tourists could see were replicas made out of polystyrene. Furthermore, that the original structure had a large flat stone roof, but when they recreated it out of polystyrene it kept blowing off, so they just left it off and edited the old photos. On another occasion some less than responsible travellers had pitched up on James's policing area and there had been a significant increase in the number of theft and anti-social behaviour reports in the surrounding environs, so in the middle of one particularly slow night shift, James and a crew mate parked nearby and threw crow-scarers into the middle of the campsite. The bangs could be heard in the town two miles away. Such 'summary justice' clearly wouldn't wash now, but 30 – 40 years ago, times were a little different.

Sadly PC James French died at an early age of cancer, but luckily I was able to attend his funeral in uniform having embarked on my own police career shortly before. His visits that inspired me to follow in his footsteps would come to the fore again in my own career later, when an appeal went out in the force for people to assist with a NSPCC campaign for people who achieved their childhood ambitions. A photograph of my Mum and me in PC French's police car, along with my story, appeared in their social media feeds in September 2015.

My uncle David Cox was also an inspiration to me, having reached the heights of Commander in the Metropolitan Police, at various points responsible for tackling serious and organised crime and establishing a 'cold-case' unit to re-examine unsolved cases. He was, and still is, supportive of my own career in policing, providing me opportunities to see him and his staff in action and providing his own stories to my family.

In September 2007, I began my policing journey, joining Nottinghamshire Police as a special constable. Specials are volunteer police officers with all the same powers as their paid counterparts. They are not PCSO's (Police Community Support Officers) who were introduced in 2002, and have only a few of the powers of a sworn constable, solely intended to be a visible presence in their community. Special constables have been around in various forms for 400 or more years and provide an invaluable contribution to policing nationally.

After six months of voluntary work, I managed to secure full-time employment with the force in a police staff role, as a call-taker within the force control room answering 999 and non-emergency calls. I continued to volunteers as a special alongside this paid role. In 2009 I managed to achieve my life's ambition and become a full-time paid police officer, a role I remained in until October 2020 when I resigned in pursuit of a new career.

Joining at the tender age of 21, I was still older than many new recruits are when they start at the age of 18, and had nearly three years of university life behind me as well as some six years working in the retail sector to have become somewhat aware of working with people.

Or so I thought.

Nothing can prepare you for the realities of police work in the 21st century – or probably any other century to be honest. I'm not ashamed of the fact that I had a fairly sheltered upbringing from 'middle-England', having only once been burgled when I was a child and never having encountered or dabbled in drugs, theft or violence. I was once stopped by the police when I worked at a newspaper shop opening up at 05:00 but was allowed on my way after offering the officers this reasonable explanation; and another occasion when I had recently passed my driving test but my brothers were still learning and so still had 'L' plates on the car –

once again, after proving my licence was fine, I was on my way. I understood that the police were doing their jobs. I may have been mildly inconvenienced for a very short time, but because I was lawfully going about my business doing nothing wrong, I was polite and courteous to them, (and they to me) I was on my way again in no time.

These two encounters and my previous life experience had not properly prepared me for what I was about to witness. Suddenly I was in a world where you can visit some people's houses and wipe your feet on the way out, hoping to scrape off the excrement from whatever mistreated pet they locked in their home for days on end. Houses where young children are still awake in the small hours of the morning watching films on the television that even most adults would shy away from. Seeing people with broken bones, or victims of domestic violence and broken lives. People who have no-one close to them and whose bodies aren't found after they commit suicide until neighbours complain of the smell or the flies coming from next door. Victims of road traffic accidents whose bodies have been mutilated beyond recognition from the nature of the collisions. The list goes on.

All these I've dealt with in my service, but I've also belly-laughed so hard with colleagues and the public that my sides have hurt. I've had high-speed pursuits and foot-chases. I've taken serious criminals off the street and ensured they receive justice, including three murderers. I've saved lives – some unquestionably through immediate action, and others I will likely never know about but for the interaction I had with them that may have changed the trajectory of their life. I hope that I've made a difference in the careers of those I've worked with, for and supervised. I've also stood up for the service I loved to be counted when it mattered. I was for a time, that focussed on my career and 'the job', that I was told by one colleague they believed if I was cut open I would bleed blue.

This book is intended to be a story of my time as a police officer in Nottinghamshire Police and specifically working in the city itself. It is a unique story, but it is also a common story. The experiences related in this book are all my own. But they are the tales of countless other officers as well. Policing is a hugely varied profession, the greatest joy of which, in my experience, comes from not knowing what each and every day will bring. Every day is different, every job is different, every person encountered is different and every colleague is different. Hopefully this book will give some insight into what a 21st century police officer deals with on the front line, in various roles, and can provide some laughs, as well as a hefty insight into the reality of possibly one of the most demanding professions in existence in the UK today.

Policing is incredibly tough, with every decision on the front line being made in split-second, real time, but open to scrutiny for hours, days, weeks, or even sometimes years afterwards. I can honestly say that 99.9% of officers that I have encountered turn up to work day-in, day-out, to try to help the communities that they serve in. They do this for relatively little money considering the dangers they face on a regular basis and the scrutiny they come under. No-one sets out to be discriminatory, violent or make mistakes. Police officers are human and they police in the society that exists, not a utopia. I can categorically tell you that no-one dislikes a corrupt police officer more than other police officers.

This unfortunate situation of accusations of racism or discriminatory behaviour can in itself lead to inaction on the part of the police; as officers are all-to-aware of the national climate. I know of one officer who chose to sustain a nasty injury, rather than use a high level of force against a violent suspect they were trying detain. The suspect was of a minority ethnicity and had the officer's force resulted in serious injury or death to the suspect, it could provoke riots or further anti-police sentiment. A colleague said of the incident that "it's a credit to those officers that they'd rather risk their lives than affect the wider public with riots etc". Quite late on in my career I once chose not to discharge my Taser at a man who was violently fighting with a colleague and me, resisting being detained for a search – largely because he was from a minority background. The news media at the time had a keen focus on police use of force against minority communities and I did not want to be the one responsible for further negative relations with different communities in Nottingham. Instead we both fought with the man for the several minutes it took for further officers to arrive. Luckily neither of us nor the man we were detaining suffered significant injuries. But these are the considerations that go through the minds of police officers, even as they are actively using all their physical and mental energy, simply to do their job. Split second decisions, that can effect entire communities, cities or countries. Damned if they do, damned if they don't.

This is both the sad reality of policing in 2020, as well as the heroic truth of the small band that refer to themselves as 'The Thin Blue Line' – "all that stand between order and chaos". To be a police officer is to be selfless and put personal feelings aside, whatever your own beliefs – whether that be removing a group of protestors from a fracking site, in spite of agreeing with their viewpoint; preventing counter protests of left- and right-wing activists from reaching one another and not demonstrating sympathy to either side; or allowing a group of protestors against supposed police brutality to walk unopposed through the main roads of the city and damage buildings, because a policing presence attempting to stop it would likely provoke disorder or make it worse. These are the kinds of decisions faced by police officers of all ranks on a daily basis and the near impossible line walked by those who choose this profession.

All this takes place in the intense glare of the public and in the ever-increasing omni-presence of camera phones, and self-styled citizen journalists, where every interaction is recorded and the most honest of mistakes splashed across news outlets. The police are eagerly and quickly judged by those who have no experience of the harsh realities faced by those who actually do it. Policing is both interesting to those outside of it (and many of those within, watching the edited highlights of their jobs!) and scrutinised heavily by the public, media and watchdogs. Police officers must accept getting filmed as part of their duties but have recently taken to doing this themselves, to present a balanced viewpoint, following the introduction of body-worn cameras. During my career I have gone viral as a result of being filmed by someone I stopped, and was also the face of the force's launch of the body worn video cameras. A clip of me being assaulted on duty the first day I was issued one was used to highlight their benefits, as one of the first such instances caught on the devices. Both of these accounts will feature in this book.

This is intended to be a largely light-hearted account of my thirteen years with Nottinghamshire Police, offering at its heart a collection of anecdotes with accompanying explanations or background information. I've mostly left out names and addresses in all but the most well-known of cases which have been in the public domain anyway. I must give a health warning however, that there are some more upsetting tales featuring descriptions of death and severe injuries. This is a large part of the role of a police officer which is why I have included them, but readers of a more sensitive disposition should probably not continue. I have also tried to steer clear of politics as much as possible, but do on occasion stray into the arena. I criticise policies and opinions, but rarely individual people and never groups. Any comprehension of my words as being discriminatory or derogatory towards any group is a misrepresentation of my intent. I have nothing but the utmost respect for every generally law-abiding member of society, many of whom are doing incredible jobs under almost impossible circumstances. I passionately stand up against those who seek to do-down the police service and sometimes perhaps this may come across as defensive or dismissive of criticism. I firmly believe there is significant room for improvement in the police (as with any organisation) and now teach new student police officers to hopefully inspire that change.

I hope this book provides some insight into the trials and tribulations faced by police officers in Nottingham in the twenty-first century and the nature of what they have to deal with. I write it for a few reasons: with my passion for history, it provides a snapshot insight of policing in the first two decades of the twenty-first century that others can look back on and study; secondly for my children, especially the youngest, who other than for pictures, can't remember me being a cop, and this is a record for them of my journey; finally for anyone else who might be interested on an inside view of the front-line of Nottingham's police force and my journey in it. I hope it is interesting to both former colleagues and outsiders equally. Most of all, I hope you enjoy it!

Tom Andrews, July 2022.

Police Emergency, What's Your Emergency?

"Well, whaddidisyeah, it's not an emergency..."

I joined paid employment with Nottinghamshire Police in the force control room answering public calls in early 2008. The force's control room is really the nerve centre of the police; where the incoming emergency and non-emergency calls are received, logged, and officers allocated to deal with them (or not). My experience of having been a special constable for about six months already, meant that I could relate the nature of the calls coming in to how they may play out in practice. This frequently manifests itself wholly differently to what the outsider may expect, and this was quite eye-opening for me in my first few months answering the calls of people at the time of the supposed crisis. My previous naivety about alternative ways of life other than my own would really come to the fore during my time here. My geography of a county of which I was not a native would also become almost encyclopaedic, although bizarrely I still don't know where most of the small, leafy, quiet villages are...

It is quite a well-established fact in policing, even if not often directly acknowledged, that what a call-taker hears on the phone or gets told by the caller, regularly does not relate to what is disclosed to the attending officers – often mere minutes later. A caller can be shouting and screaming down the phone to "get the police here now" because they're being attacked or want someone out the house who is refusing to leave; but when officers actually arrive, everyone is calm and best of friends again, instead swearing at the officers to leave. Similarly common is for callers to be shouting at the call-taker that they're being assaulted, someone won't leave, or is being abusive, and you can hear the other person in the background coolly and calmly saying "no I'm not, I'm just sat here."

Every call is taken at face value and every caller is believed until it becomes clear that there is contradictory evidence. Crime recording (figures collated by the government and released to te public to show 'crime rates') is based on this initial report, and not necessarily what is said to officers later. This can often result in formal crimes being recorded by the ' data compliance team' which are not related to the experience of the officers on the ground. This however is what the Home Office require, based on the view that the caller is most likely to disclose the basic circumstances at the point that they are motivated to call the police – however far-fetched that report may be. Crime rates in the last few years have risen, against a previous general downward trend. This is why. On more than one occasion I saw a crime report for 'rape' generated because a male caller rang in to report that a woman he had fallen out with was threatening to falsely report that he'd raped her. She never rang in, but because the man reported that she was alleging it, the allegation was recorded 'for statistical purposes' as a crime with him as the named suspect. There's irony for you.

It is also not unusual for people to exaggerate their situation to get a quicker police response. A 'routine' call reporting youths being noisy on the street may get you the attendance of a police officer – or more likely PCSO or council warden – at some time in the next few hours. If those youths "have a knife" then you are guaranteed police attendance within minutes. Unfortunately many regular or persistent callers know this and will report issues to be far bigger than they actually are. The ambulance service suffer the same with their regular callers suffering "breathing difficulties" or "chest pain" to get a faster response. A regular police call may go along these lines:

Call Handler: "Police Emergency, what's the emergency?"

Caller: "There's a group of youths on my street and I think one of them has a knife"

Call Handler: "Can you describe the knife to me?"

Caller: "Yes, he's taken it out his pocket, and showing it around. It's shiny in his hand."

Call Handler: "OK, there's officers on their way to you now, equipped with Taser. Can you describe the one with the knife?"

Caller: "Well, I *think* it *might* be a knife. He's definitely got something shiny in his hand. He's a young male wearing all black clothing. There's three of them. They're all shouting about something."

Call Handler: "OK, about the knife, is it a kitchen knife, lock knife, can you describe it more?"

Caller: "Well, erm, it could be a bottle actually, now I can see better. It's definitely glinting in the light though. And they're all shouting loudly at something. They've been out here for ages now doing it."

Obviously valuable police resources are allocated to these sorts of incidents, especially highly trained Taser or firearms officers who are an even more scarce resource, for what invariably turns out to be anti-social behaviour. This type of call puts people's lives at risk, both from the officers travelling at high speed on blue lights to get to the scene quickly, or taking those resources away from other actually more serious incidents for the time that they are dealing with this one. Whether there is genuine intent on the caller's part to mislead the police to get a faster response, or an honest held belief it was a knife or weapon and they dialled in haste and it turns out otherwise is anyone's guess. There are however calls where the reporters are demonstrable liars.

***

For a period of a month or so, there was a series of burglary-in-progress calls to some addresses in a student area of the city. These types of calls attract all available officers to attend from wherever they may be – everyone joins the job to catch burglars and few ever lose that passion. It's an abhorrent crime, so to catch one in the act is one of the best feelings you can get. Officers were sent to the calls, which generally came in along the lines of "the house near mine is empty currently, and I can see movement inside it". These would attract several police units, all attending on blue lights, driving perhaps that little bit faster to get the burglar before they leave. Every time the first officers arrived though, it would turn out that the person in the address was a builder, renovating the house ready for students to move in. The builder did keep slightly odd hours – doing the renovations to this, their own property, after their normal working hours for paying customers. It turned out that the caller did not appreciate the odd hours kept by the builder, or apparently that the house would be for students, and so reported it to the police in the manner they did to ensure a police response.

Call-handlers and the radio dispatchers can see previous calls, both from a caller's phone number and to the address being attended. When it's a call to a burglary currently taking place though, the call handler will generally keep the caller on the line and get us much information as they can, and officers can be on scene in a matter of two to three minutes from the call being made if they are nearby. This doesn't give time for these normal background checks to be made.

These calls went on for three or four nights in a row. Every time they received the same large and prompt police response for what was essentially a complaint about anti-social working hours. A complaint that should have been made to the council or trading standards.

What became of the caller, I don't know. This isn't uncommon when answering calls as you move onto the next one as soon as you hang up the phone, and on-going investigations are run on a different system – but I would hope they were dealt with for wasting police time.

***

Perhaps the biggest lie of all is the large number of people who ring 999, and conversations go like this

Call handler: "Police emergency, what's your emergency?"

Caller: "Well, whaddidisyeah, it's not an emergency, but I haven't got any credit..."

This is a sad reflection of today's society and of a large number of the callers to the police. It's suggestive of an endemic issue that those most frequently wanting to report issues to the police are also those who most regularly claim to have no credit to report what are often fairly trivial matters. It demonstrates a high sense of selfishness, that instead of waiting until they have a few pence credit on their phone, they would rather potentially put another (unknown) person's life in danger by taking up a 999 line.

When I first started in the control room we were allowed to tell the callers that they were ringing on an emergency line and that we couldn't take their report unless they did it via the correct manner of the non-emergency number. It wasn't long after I left that that policy changed and now the call-handlers are expected to 'offer advice' to those misusing the 999 system, but to take the report anyway. The rights or wrongs of this policy change are not for me to discuss, but you are the reader are entirely able to form your own opinions. All I would say is that those doing it are those that have probably had endless 'advice' throughout their lives on various matters, and heeded none of it.

Sadly most of the calls that misuse the 999 system are by those who clearly aren't reporting anything remotely like something resembling an emergency. There are some people who ring 999 when they return home from work and discover that their house has been broken into . This is a horrible situation to find yourself in and the last thing you're thinking about is which specific number for the police that you ought to be ringing. For me, people who ring 999 to report finding their house having been ransacked are entirely justified in doing so, even though there isn't a crime happening now *per se*. Sadly the majority of people who misuse the 999 system, especially those who begin with the "I've got no credit..." line, are ringing to report pointlessly trivial incidents, for which the police really ought to never be involved. The kind of incidents that before the advent of the digital and social media age would have simply been shrugged off or at the worst resulted in some kind of verbal argument.

Now, with the advent of free and quick electronic communications, people feel the overriding need to send insults to one another via all manner of electronic methods. The 999 calls that begin with the 'lack of credit' clause normally continue along this vein:

Call handler: "You really shouldn't be ringing 999 just because you haven't got phone credit. Is there something urgent that you need to report?"

Caller: "Well, whaddidisyeah, it's not an emergency right, but ma sister's boyfriend's cousin's called me a slag on Facebook, and basically, yeah, if yous lot don't do somefink 'bout it I'm gunna go round there and bang her out, filthy little sket. So basically it is an emergency cos I'm gunna go round there naa."

(Translation: "Someone who I don't really know has said some hurty words to me online and now I'm going to tell you that I'm going to dramatically over-react to the situation in order to force your hand to become involved, and sooner rather than later". I've it written as it would be spoken in a colloquial Nottingham accent.)

I'm not really sure what makes people think it's OK to ring a life or death emergency line to report that someone they've probably rarely, if ever, met has called them something derogatory on social media. Even more so when they then follow that up with qualified threats of violence themselves. There are numerous police stations with front counters to report things, there is online reporting, or even the option (heaven forbid) of just getting over it... These types of callers are sadly all too common and unfortunately the *Malicious Communications* Act which hails from the very pre-social media age of 1988, contains an offence of "sending a message which is grossly indecent or offensive; a threat; or information which is known to be false by the sender."

Unfortunately this makes the issue of calling someone a "slag" via the delightful medium of social media a criminal offence. That means that not only do the call handlers have to log an incident requiring some kind of police action, but that the call will generate a crime 'number' – a formal notification to the government that a crime has occurred. This one crime number carries the same numerical weight as the one crime number generated for a murder or carrying a firearm. A police officer will be dispatched to deal with the sender of the "slag" message, and also have to offer words of advice to the caller about making indirect threats to other people. This advice is *always* well received by the recipients, and nine times out of ten the alleged offender will show a chain of messages where the original caller has called the supposed offender far worse than a slag, resulting in that original caller being subject of a crime report as well. Two for the price of one.

A most valid use of the telephone system designed to save lives.

And, sure as night follows day, both parties will then be slating the police on the same social media platforms that "they should be dealing with more important things, like catching rapists and murderers". *C'est la vie.*

***

Answering the phones is in equal parts mundane on occasion as it is terrifying on others. Occasionally there were calls that would stay with you for a very long time, if not forever. The nature of the role of answering emergency calls means that what is 'another day at the office' for the call handler is quite possibly the biggest crisis ever faced by the person at the other end of the line.

Officers may have to deal with the situation in person, but they won't arrive until at least a few minutes later. It is also often easier to process and deal with, as when they are physically there they can influence the situation. They also get closure by knowing the outcome of the incident. To a large extent all the call handler can do is listen and offer some small advice. In the middle of often acute hysteria or crisis their job is to get the location of the caller at the very least in order to send police officers. One of the most harrowing calls I ever took was a situation where even that wasn't possible.

The BT 999 operator ("Which service do you require?") put a call through and explained that they could hear heavy breathing and what sounded like someone asking for help. Protocol in this situation with no direct requests is to put calls to the police, as they hold the most information in the form of intelligence to hopefully be able to trace the caller. Police officers are all first aid trained and carry fire extinguishers in their cars so can also deal with a majority of situations. The call was put through and indeed faintly I could hear the words "help" and someone who sounded like they were struggling to breathe.

After several minutes of trying to get any information at all I wasn't able to. It was obvious from the wind noise in the background that the caller was outside. All I could work out was that the person sounded like a woman and the information of which mobile phone mast their call had routed through. Conducting checks on the phone number whilst trying to speak to the caller only yielded that the caller was likely to be a lady who lived in the vicinity of the phone mast, but that didn't help greatly, given the fact that she appeared to be outside.

Several police units were assigned to start searching the area and it was another few minutes before I heard a male voice in the background asking "are you OK?". A passing pedestrian had chanced across the elderly woman caller who'd collapsed on the floor. I was able to get his attention, get their location, divert the police officers to them and request an ambulance. As far as I know the woman made a full recovery. The knowledge after the fact, or often not knowing the full outcome, does nothing to diminish the anxiety that is caused by the original call and knowing that someone needs your help, but that you can't help them. Thankfully this turned out to be a relatively minor first-aid incident, but the pleas for help and not being able to arrange that was more then enough to cause some quite intense worry on my part.

***

Dealing with life or death situations can be traumatic, even when at the other end of a phone call. I was at work one evening when a colleague received a call that stayed with them for life and resulted in them needing counselling themselves.

When a particularly serious call came in, colleagues sat near to the operator taking it could soon pick this up from the tone of their co-worker's voice and nature of what they were saying. They could then monitor the computer log as it was being created and assist in any way they could. This was one such occasion, where it became apparent that my colleague was on a call to a person suffering an acute mental health crisis. Finding the incident log as it was coming in, I saw that the caller was saying they were in the middle of a wood, stood on a tree branch with a rope round their neck, intending to jump. They had called police to tell us where they were, so we could find their body, but that nothing we could do would stop them going through with their intention.

Sure enough, as I heard my colleague negotiating and pleading with the caller, I could hear their voice change and the look on their face turn to horror as it became apparent the caller had indeed jumped and my colleague was listening to them dying, as the phone had fallen out of the caller's hand onto the floor with the line still open.

Police officers arrived within minutes and commenced CPR, with an ambulance arriving soon after. I honestly can't remember whether the caller lived, but I think that they did, and hopefully found the help that they needed.

This incident, along with the other similarly disturbing calls regularly received, meant that that colleague ultimately suffered with their own mental health concerns. This isn't uncommon for police call handlers, but counselling services are available and they are reasonably well supported by the organisation and staff unions. Sadly, an ever-increasing number of calls for service to the police are mental health related. In 2015 the College of Policing estimated that between 20 – 40% of police demand was related to mental health in some way, and that figure has surely risen since then.[*] Police officers and staff are not immune to mental health problems either, especially considering the trauma that they face and I will look at this a bit more later on. The control room however has one of the highest instances of mental health related sickness in the police, probably for all the reasons outlined in this chapter: a lack of being able to directly intervene; speaking to people at their most

---

[*] https://www.college.police.uk/News/College-news/Documents/Demand%20Report%2023_1_15_noBleed.pdf#search=estimating%20demand

acute moment of crisis; a lack of 'closure' about what happened to the callers after the phone was hung up; and listening to serious injury or death on the phone; as well as long hours of 24/7 shift work impacting on sleep and wellbeing.

The solution to this is not for me to analyse here and is probably a good topic for someone studying a Master's or PhD, but my experience is that police chiefs do not take the problem of mental health concerns and wellbeing of their staff seriously enough. Thankfully this is something that the Police Federation, staff unions and external charities are actively raising on a national level as I am writing this.

***

Equally as haunting as listening to someone suffering a mental health crisis, is listening to someone in absolute, abject fear. The most common manifestations of these calls are in domestic violence situations, where for example a man is either battering the female caller, or kicking the door down to get into her address. The victim (and they are a victim at this point, they're not yet a survivor – as people who have come out the other side of domestic abuse are more appropriately referred to) will call police and be screaming down the phone to get the officers there as quickly as possible.

Trying to type the relevant information into the correct fields on the command-and-control system to get the incident created, so officers can attend as soon as possible, becomes almost a superhuman achievement. There is a real skill answering emergency calls in remaining calm and getting the required information out of the victim. There is also a massive credit due to the callers in these types of situation. They are at a point where their only potential hope of salvation in that moment of terror, is the call handler at the other end of the phone. Somehow they are able to be strong enough to listen to the questions the call handler is asking them and give answers, all whilst they know full well that there is someone intent on causing them serious harm trying to get to them. Their bravery in these situations is to be commended.

In dangerous potentially violent situations like this call handlers will stay on the phone with the caller until the police arrive. This acts both as reassurance for the caller and someone to talk to, as well as serving as an opportunity to capture potential evidence on the audio recording. That evidence comes in the form of hearing the incident unfold. I have heard far too many people being beaten, burgled and berated. The worst noise is the sound of objects being used as weapons to hit people and you are powerless to intervene. Usually there is also great relief at the sound of the 'cavalry' arriving as 'those in blue' turn up at the address. You hope that what you heard on the call will later be heard by the courts and result in a decent sentence for the offender. Sadly too often that's not the case.

***

I have already highlighted one such instance, but the police are frequently used a first point of contact for people in mental health crisis. There are numerous more suitable agencies for dealing with people suffering from breakdowns or relapses, but too many of these are only available in office hours or don't come out to see people, only help over the phone. This is not necessarily their fault and funding for mental health facilities has been cut drastically over the recent years. People in moments of crisis know that by ringing the police we can attend immediately and provide assistance. Similarly, it may not be the patient ringing, but a family member at their wit's end trying to restrain or calm down their relative but unable to do so; or members of the public who have encountered someone having an episode in the street.

There are several different types of caller to the police with mental health concerns. There are obviously those as described above who are in crisis and genuinely need help in any form at that very moment. There are numerous others however, that fall into a couple of different categories.

There are the regular persistent callers. One example from my time answering calls would ring four or five times a day if not more and wish to report very similar things:

- Her carers were taking money (small amounts) from her purse.
- The police were harassing her.
- She had been burgled and a piece of paperwork had been taken.
- Her neighbours were planning a terrorist attack.

She would not ring on 999, but the calls are answered by the same people in the same room, and whilst 999 calls take priority over non-emergency calls, if everyone is on a call the 999 callers have to wait. Answering the phone to persistent callers such as this takes up a not inconsiderable part of the day. The issue is that they are genuinely unwell; they absolutely believe what they are reporting and it is not in anyone's interest to criminalise them. In extreme cases some callers of this ilk are given injunctions and for the most part they understand these and the condition to only contact the police in an emergency. These take time to obtain though, and the majority of the calls are filtered out by the call handlers who are very familiar with the persistent callers and the nature of their regular false reports. They're often visited by the local neighbourhood officers as well to ensure they are safe and well, and social services referrals are made for longer term support. The other ironic aspect about these calls is that under the above mentioned Home Office rules, as these are reports of a crime having taken place, unless there is demonstrable evidence to the contrary, they have to be formally recorded. It is insufficient to say that because the caller suffers from adverse mental health conditions the crimes haven't happened (and of course, this should *never* be a reason to not believe a report). This caller was therefore almost single-handedly responsible for a hyper-local crimewave in her house, which obviously never resulted in a 'suspect' being identified, let alone caught and subsequently lowering 'detection' rates.

One of our regular callers was a lovely lady who was always really friendly on the phone, and would often even admit that she was just phoning for a chat. It's difficult to terminate these calls overly quickly from persistent callers, as you don't want to be rude to them. In most cases they are just lonely, or genuinely believe that they are reporting a crime. This was even more the case for this particular lady given how polite and friendly she was – she had even changed her name to include 'Queen' as a prefix, so outgoing was she. She'd often end the calls by asking us to get the local officers to pop round and see her where she would have boxes of chocolate for them to take back to the station. I found out later that one time an officer did go round to take her up on the offer, but on seeing her, the 'chocolates' turned out to be something else 'brown and sticky'... Luckily the officer could tell something wasn't right from their dubious smell prior to taste-testing them, and the no doubt well-intentioned gift was declined...

There were also callers whose conditions manifested by ringing the police and shouting the foulest abuse at the call takers. I have been called all manner of insults, based on race, sexual orientation, beliefs and gender. Luckily it is very apparent when the caller is suffering from a mental ailment, and the insults generally wash off like water from a duck's back.

Other callers suffering mental health conditions are those who have somehow slipped through the cracks and have escaped notice from public agencies and have no family or friends checking on them either. These are often very tragic and even horrific, such as the occasion where one such caller rang the police asking for help as there were "snakes crawling around his living room and blood everywhere". Given the nature of the call, and no previous call history from the address or number, officers attended promptly. On their arrival it transpired that the male had been neglected for some not inconsiderable time and become quite unwell. A large tapeworm had come out from his digestive tract (I'll leave the explicit details to your imagination), crawled across the living room and behind the curtains, which also accounted for the large amount of blood that was present. An ambulance was hastily called and the man taken to hospital; social services and other relevant agencies were all notified. Sadly once again I don't know the outcome of this particular tale, but the actions of the public agencies involved would have ensured he had the best possible chance at a better life.

This was the first glimpse for me into the concerns around vulnerability that now weave a thread through almost all policing activity. A significant percentage of police encounters today involve someone who is vulnerable in some way; whether that be through drink / drugs, circumstance, prior life experiences, physical or mental health, or a variety of other reasons. Vulnerability and the police response to it is probably the biggest issue facing policing in the 21st century. It is clear from successive inquiries into tragic circumstances like Victoria Climbié, Baby Peter, Fiona Pilkington and countless others that the public expect the police and other public bodies to do all they can, working together, to help vulnerable people. This was not the case when I was answering the phones, and the concept of vulnerability as such a significant issue was probably only just starting to come to the fore. It was to be a recurring theme throughout my later policing career though, and continues to be an ever increasing part of what the police service are expected to respond to in today's climate. There is a painstakingly gradual but hugely important shift away from the idea that people solely commit crime through greed. There is now far more of an understanding that vulnerability plays a huge role in the underlying causes of supposed criminality and it is not actually a conscious choice on the parts of many suspects who are accused of more minor crimes. There are some staggering statistics that show if you experience trauma in childhood that as an adult you are between 4 – 12 times more likely to become an addict of drink or drugs, suffer from depression or attempt suicide; up to 4 times more likely to smoke or have poor health; and have more than 50 sexual partners, be unable to hold down relationships and contract sexually transmitted diseases.* This shows that many of those who commit crimes don't do so out of choice – it's a result their upbringing and psychology.

Call handlers have a very unenviable job, but they are all unsung heroes, as the first people that those in need of help speak to. They

---

* Felitti et al. (1998) 'Relationship of Childhood Abuse and Household Dysfunction to Many of the Leading Causes of Death in Adults: The Adverse Childhood Experiences (ACE) *Study' American Journal of Preventive Medicine*, Vol. 14, No. 4 pp.245-258 overview available at: https://www.ajpmonline.org/article/S0749-3797(98)00017-8/abstract

have an almost unique opportunity to counsel those who call the police actually in the very moment of their crisis. I thoroughly enjoyed my time in the force control room and I feel it is an excellent insight into the world of policing. If I were put in charge of police training, I would make it mandatory for all new recruits to spend several months answering calls. This would give them an excellent understanding of the difficult role the call handlers face, translating incoherent shouting for help into something that can be passed to officers. More importantly is would give them an unparalleled insight into the broad nature of what different sections of the public actually expect from the police, and the types of incidents that have to get created. It certainly opened my eyes to the fact that policing is far more than 'cops and robbers'.

Hitting the Beat

"You'll never take me alive, coppers!"

In late May 2009 I started training as a paid full time police officer. Starting this role was a tale in itself, as I'd been given a starting date of early March and even met all my new colleagues from that training intake and had my welcome induction day. I'd handed my notice in to the control room, but was informed a fortnight before beginning my training that I couldn't actually start on the date advised. This stemmed from a complaint I had received as a special constable that was still under investigation.

The complaint itself had originated in the middle of 2008, when working as a special with the city centre pro-active team, doing a Friday evening shift policing the 'Night Time Economy'. Whilst patrolling in the van, the driver and front seat passenger had seen a car pull out of a junction in front of us, forcing the van to brake hard, and the car had no lights on – tell-tale signs of a drink driver. On went the blue lights and the car pulled over. I and two others went to speak to the driver and sure enough other apparent signs of alcohol consumption were present. One of the cops requested a breath sample from the driver who blew over the limit and was promptly arrested.

He was put into the cage of the police van for transport to the custody suite, but on-route he stopped talking and slumped down in the cell. I was watching him from in the back of the van so I opened the internal door to get to him and tested his reactions, including flinch reaction, which was fine. Unconscious people don't feel pain, but if you're even remotely conscious, a small pinch of the earlobe always provokes a squirm, It's not intended to cause pain, but is used by police and paramedics alike to test for a reaction. He was also breathing with no difficulty, albeit maybe a little quick. I passed all this information to my more experienced colleagues who also checked on him and agreed that he was fine. We arrived at custody where he wouldn't get out the van, so we carried him into a spacious fish-tank-like 'holding cell' so we could watch him, and requested the resident custody nurse check him out. There's a nurse stationed in the custody suite at all times so they were able to come straight to see him and also concurred that he was absolutely fine and was simply faking it.

This isn't an uncommon tactic for people arrested on suspicion of drink-driving, as they try any number of tricks to delay having to give an evidential breath sample in the hope they lose alcohol in their system and then blow under the limit. The opinion of the nurse in this instance, supported by all their equipment readings and experience, was that this was exactly what was happening.

One of the full-time officers then conducted a formal drink-drive procedure with the arrested chap who continued not to respond and therefore failed to provide a sample. He continued to not open his eyes and was lolling his head, so an ambulance was called to be on the safe side. Policing is a surprisingly risk-averse profession. The paramedics arrived and they reached the same conclusion as the nurse and ourselves. He was taken to hospital anyway and lo-and-behold, no sooner had we arrived and the chap put onto a bed, he 'came round' and made a miraculous recovery. To such an extent that he discharged himself after an hour or so, but only after he'd been charged with failing to provide a sample of breath and bailed from police custody.

He subsequently made a formal complaint about the incident, stating that he had been mistreated when suffering a medical emergency and not believed. The irony being that if he were having a genuine medical emergency, he would not have known that he was not believed, as he initially claimed in the hospital to remember nothing from the time he was arrested to 'coming around' there. The nature of police complaints however means they cannot be concluded until any criminal proceedings are completed. The male pleaded 'not guilty' to his charge and so a full trial was needed, which at that time was about a six month wait. The trial got postponed, so added a further two months delay. When it happened, all seven officers including myself had to give evidence, as did the custody nurse, the paramedics and the nurse at the hospital – all giving evidence that he was displaying no medical signs of being ill. He was perhaps unsurprisingly found guilty of failing to provide a breath sample and the complaint was then concluded, obviously finding no wrongdoing on the parts of the officers involved.

This had concluded about a month before I was due to start, so this is when I had my induction session and met all my course mates. I was then notified that the complainant had appealed the decision, prompting a review by the Independent Police Complaints Commission (IPCC). They reviewed the investigation reasonably expeditiously and concurred with the Professional Standards Department (responsible for investigating complaints and misconduct by police officers) investigation. Due to this appeal going to the IPCC however, I was notified that I was unable to start in my paid role, still being subject to active disciplinary proceedings. Luckily I was allowed to postpone my leaving the control room. The IPCC investigation and his 28-day right to appeal that decision delayed my start from early March to the next intake in late May. The complainant did not appeal the IPCC decision and I was finally allowed to start in my dream career on 26th May 2009. Fortunately at that time there was a large scale recruitment happening, so my start was not delayed excessively. Most other years, I would have been waiting another year for the next intake.

This was not to be my first encounter with the Professional Standards Department (PSD), who serve almost as a 'bogey-man' to officers. Sadly there is a clear need for a team of people to investigate misconduct in the police, but it is the experience of many officers that on occasion the PSD overstep the bounds of what is actually needed or appropriate. There will be further examples of my encounters with the PSD as time progresses, but I have had more negative experiences with them than positive. I myself have never faced disciplinary proceedings or had any negative outcomes, but the manner in which they have conducted themselves when I have had dealings with them as the subject of a complaint, or as a witness, has left a lot to be desired. The ethos of the department improved significantly in the last few years of my career, noticeably as Craig Guildford took over as Chief Constable in Nottinghamshire and with it the national portfolio of professional standards. He transformed the culture of the PSD from being punitive to educational, and with it reduced the climate of fear that the department had held previously. Sadly though for the first half of my career the attitude of the PSD can be summed up with a quote that a police staff member was overheard to say when they found out they were successful in applying for a role on the PSD – "Great, now I can have cops fired.".

***

After successfully navigating the complaint issue and completing my training I joined an emergency response team at

Central Police Station, which at that time covered the City Centre, as well as the inner-city areas of Lenton and Radford. The emergency response team is best described as the front-line uniformed cops who turn up if you ring the police to report an incident. Several incidents during my tutorship phase have stuck with me, serving as eye-openers to what I had signed up for.

I started in November, after six months in training school learning law, self-defence, computer systems and policies. This meant that I was being tutored over the Christmas and New Year period and my shift were actually on duty on New Year's Eve that year. Due to the numbers of officers in from my shift and another shift who had had their day off cancelled to provide extra staffing, we all went out in threes due to a lack of cars and dozens of officers already deployed on foot in the city. I was with my tutor and another fairly young-in-service officer.

New Year's Eves are bizarre, as in spite of huge numbers of people being out, there is very little going on from a policing point of view until around 01:00 or 02:00 in the morning. Everyone stays well behaved to see in the New Year and only then hits the drink. Calls to fights and other incidents often continue coming in until 08:00 or 09:00 in the morning. This particular night, we saw in the stroke of midnight parked outside Nottingham Castle, both to ensure public safety there as well as watch the fireworks. The night then picked up and one of our first calls was to a report of a minor disturbance at a pub in Radford. We went on our own, with three of us being confident of breaking up a small dispute. On our arrival we were confronted with a scene of chaos, the whole premises had erupted and a full blown 'pub fight' was occurring – chairs and bottles were being thrown and fists were swinging everywhere. Following a hasty request for some additional officers the three of us waded into the scene of carnage. I made a beeline for a group I saw fighting on a small stage area and started attempting to separate them.

The odd thing about being a police officer, is that oftentimes no matter what dispute people are having with one another, as soon as you arrive to try and resolve it, all those involved suddenly become friends again and round on you! This happened here and both parties started advancing towards me; so remembering my newly learnt self-defence tactics I used my arms to forcibly push back one of the women who was storming at me, in order to create some space. Unfortunately, as we were on a raised platform and she had consumed a fair amount of drink, she went flying backwards off the stage straight onto a wooden table which promptly collapsed underneath her, like something straight out of a Hollywood Western. For a split second I thought I'd caused her serious injury and saw my very brief career coming to a hasty end. Luckily less than a second later the woman got straight back up and began to shout and swear at me. I've never been happier before or since to face a barrage of abuse! As a bonus, not only was she fine, but she didn't fancy her chances trying to get to me again either, content instead to stay where she was and gesticulate angrily at me.

Several back-up vans full of officers arrived after a couple of minutes and the pub was cleared out with no arrests made and no-one suffering serious injuries. The pub itself closed down long ago and full-scale pub fights like this happen rarely if ever now thanks to CCTV and strict licensing enforcement. The adrenaline rush and sense of abject fear from being one of the first officers on scene to a large disorder like that is something to be reckoned with though, but luckily isn't something experienced very often.

Later that same night we had been to a report of domestic violence and were taking the victim to their parents' house in the Sneinton area of the city. This was on a different police radio channel to the city centre, and being the new and keen officer straight from the control room where everything revolved around the radio and calls, I switched to the local channel. My other colleague didn't though as we were only going to be there a short time. My tutor took the victim into the address to speak to them and ensure they were safe, whilst my colleague and I remained in the car. Suddenly there was a knock on the window and a man told us that there was a large fight on the next street. We got out and ran over, and sure enough there's about 15 people fighting in the middle of the main road, some with planks of wood in their hands, and no doubt some other makeshift or intended weapons.

I requested more officers on the local radio channel I'd switched to, but my colleague hit his emergency button. This little red button on the top of the radios cuts out any other radio traffic and makes a noise in the ear of every other officer that is instantly recognisable as an officer needing urgent assistance. It also allows the person activating it to talk uninterrupted for a short period without having to press the push-to-talk button. He was still on the city centre radio channel though and to top it off after hitting the button, his earpiece came out in the scuffle, so he couldn't hear anything being asked of him, such as his location or what was happening. I'd let local officers know the situation and they were travelling to us with blue lights on, but my tutor who was in the house with the victim heard our other colleague's emergency activation and ran outside. She couldn't find us as we weren't in the car where she left us. Luckily the radio operators for the two radio channels sit next to each other in the control room so were quickly able to work out that what I was requesting additional officers for was the same incident that my colleague had activated his emergency button for. Other officers arrived quickly and the situation was quickly resolved with several arrests made. Thankfully large street fights like this are not common, and it was probably a combination off too much alcohol, excitement and maybe a suspicion that the police would be too busy in town to deal with something in a suburb.

***

New Year's Eves are one of the most simple nights to work and also one of the most enjoyable, as there are normally enough resources to deal with anything and everything that might occur. The nature of the incidents is also fairly simple – predominantly consisting of drunken fights and criminal damage. There's not always enough resources though or occasionally things can go wrong, and the one year I worked New Year's Eve in the control room the new command-and-control system the force had just invested in crashed, meaning we had to record everything on paper. This created huge delays and for several hours we had dozens of 999 calls showing as still waiting to be answered, never mind the non-emergency calls. When this happens, if there are excessive delays in answering a 999 call, neighbouring forces and those further afield start answering the calls and then (at that time) faxed them through to us, so we were not only answering as many calls as we could, but having to receive faxes from other forces across the country who were answering our calls.

I'll never forget the Chief Inspector who was in charge of the 'contact management' department at that time, Sean, was working that night to oversee the whole New Years' Eve policing operation. When things really 'hit the fan' he came and sat down next to me, put a headset on and started answering phone calls himself. This was inspirational to those of us sat near him, as this sort of thing never happened. He may not have had a lot of the relevant training or daily experience that generates the muscle memory and intuition, but he still wanted to play his part and help however he could. He was one of the best bosses I ever worked for and he nominated me for my first ever commendation, and his development of people was second to none. I was to encounter him many times throughout my ongoing policing career until he retired a couple of years ago. It was this 'hands-on' style of leadership that stuck with me and that I used myself when I took supervisory roles. I have always found that when leaders, of whatever seniority, work 'on the factory floor' as such, it does untold wonders for morale and respect from those doing the role. It was a strategy used very well by the Chief Constable Craig Guildford when he joined the force later in my service.

***

It's not just New Years' Eves that can be busy, the whole Christmas period can be a time that makes people act strangely – whether due to alcohol or depression or myriad other factors. It was Christmas Eve a year or two into my service when I was on an afternoon shift and due to finish at 23:00. For our last job of the shift, two colleagues and I were requested to attend a block of flats in Radford. This was passed to us as a 'safe and well' check on a man who had made threats to his social worker. He'd apparently said that he intended to set his own flat on fire because he wanted to be moved somewhere else and felt that he hadn't received adequate help from social care or housing support. We arrived and knocked on the flat door. There was no reply so I opened the letterbox to shout through, at which point I noticed a distinct smell of burning.

I put my hand to the glass in the front door, which was hot to the touch – the inside of the flat was obviously on fire! We urgently requested extra police officers and the fire brigade to join us.

At this time we didn't know whether the man was inside the flat or not. The council owned the building which thankfully meant it had CCTV in the hallways, so we requested that they urgently reviewed the footage whilst we began attempting to kick the door in. We didn't have an 'enforcer' (battering ram) with us so the three of us took turns frantically kicking at the door using various techniques, eventually succeeding in breaking it down. Confronting us inside in the corridor was a wall of thick acrid black smoke, stretching from ceiling down to knee height.

It was quite something witnessing the early stages of a house fire. Nothing compares to the denseness of that thick black smoke that was impossible to see through and appeared to be floating in the air from the ceiling down. It was something I'd never seen before and I remember being quite surprised at how thick and impenetrable it looked, especially in comparison to the still clear air below knee height. And also how it came from the ceiling down, rather than like dry ice smoke, which clings to the floor. If anything, it has made me always remember the advice if you're ever in a fire to stay as low as possible.

The level of concern about the possibility of a person being inside that flat still is difficult to convey. It was one of those moments that you think would only ever happen in Hollywood movies, where emergency services staff have to potentially run into a burning building to save someone. *This was that moment*, happening in real life, and it was both terrifying and accelerating at the same time.

After a brief discussion between the three of us, we concluded that we needed to at least try to check to see if the male was in there. The last information the social worker had got from the man was that he was heading home, and his threats had specifically included staying in the flat when he set it on fire. The first duty of a police officer is to preserve life and limb, so we all reached the conclusion that we were at least going to have to try to go into the burning flat. We were faced with that horrifying prospect, made worse by the fact that if he was in there, it was likely intentional, and he would probably refuse to come out with us willingly.

I took off my fleece and put it over my mouth to protect it as best as possible from the foul-smelling toxic fumes, and entered the corridor. The smoke was so dense that I couldn't get more than a few feet into the corridor before I was unable to see anything and started struggling to breathe. Even attempting to 'commando crawl' along the corridor underneath the visible smoke, I could taste the fumes in my throat and my eyes were watering. After a few shouts to anyone who might have been in there and getting no reply, I had to beat a hasty retreat. Even as I got back to the external landing area the smoke was getting lower and lower to the floor and nearly filled from floor to ceiling.

Realising we were not going to be able to get into the flat we immediately started evacuating the entire building. One of my colleagues tripped the fire alarm and we started going door-to-door hammering and shouting as loudly as we could to get the residents out. It was late evening so parents were having to wake children up and grab whatever they might need, having no idea how long they would be out their homes for.

As more officers began arriving the three of us were directing each newly arriving officer to where they needed to start evacuating residents from or close roads, as well as doing the same ourselves.

Luckily the night shift had just started coming into work for their shift so they all headed down to us as well to assist.

This is typical of the mindset of police officers who will happily turn out to serious incidents before their actual shift starts, or attend them late on where they know it will make them late off. Those who complain about police officers taking ages to arrive at their reported incident probably aren't reporting something that needs a substantial urgent response. I have never known a time where at least one officer can't or won't make themselves available for situations that *really* need them. There are of course occasions where the police force *do* genuinely run out of available resources. Even then if there is a person that drastically needs an officer as soon as possible due to some great immediate risk, a cop will often resume from whatever they're already dealing with, even if it means they will be late off or receive a complaint from the person that they've left. They would rather that the person in need of immediate help gets that. This is the nature of most officers and this professionalism is done no favours by the constant media barrage of criticism suggesting they're lazy or don't care. One day, probably soon, the public will reap what the media have sewn and police officers will lose this selflessness, choosing instead to just 'clock-on' and 'clock-off'. That will be a sad day indeed.*

The fire service arrived at the scene within a matter of minutes, ran their hoses up to the flat and started getting water on the building. My colleagues and I managed to get all the residents we could account for out of the building and I finally managed to take stock of the situation. Looking up at the flats from the road outside

---

* Post-script, as I review this for publishing, Police Scotland have announced a 'withdrawal of goodwill' exactly as described, as a result of poor pay and conditions.

I could see that the fire had by now firmly taken hold and flames were licking out and around the ceilings of the external walkways, curling round the roof, along almost the entire top floor of the three-storey building. The fire brigade told me that the fire had spread into the roof space, and it took some eight appliances and several hours to get the fire under control.

The poor residents of the flats not only had much of their property soaked from the water poured onto the fire by the gallon, or burnt from the fire, but also had to spend that night and the next day – Christmas Day no less – in the sports hall of a nearby school, with some having to spend several more days put up in hotels as well.

The CCTV playback ultimately showed that the man responsible had left the flat mere minutes before our arrival. He was promptly located by the CID, arrested and convicted of Arson with Intent to Endanger Life and sent to prison for many years. Every year on Christmas Day I always think of those poor families who were the innocent victims forced into emergency accommodation. It all stemmed from the selfish actions of one person's dissatisfaction with the speed of a response from public services that impacted on so many. But then, like so many, he was also probably battling with his own personal demons – after all, what person of fully sound mind would consider his actions as a remotely rational response to his situation.

***

In another example of officers going the extra mile, this time myself, the following year on Boxing Day I'd enjoyed a rare

Christmas period off work but was due back in on 27th. I'd been to see my parents who lived in Plymouth at the time and was heading back up the M5 on Boxing Day afternoon. Just prior to reaching Bristol I rounded a bend to be confronted by a car side-on, upside-down in the inside lane. There was one other car stopped who was obviously on the phone to the emergency services, so I stopped and positioned my car to shield the stranded car and ran back down the road to put a hazard warning triangle out as far in advance as I could – it's aways important to protect yourself before treating any casualties lest you become one as well. Returning to the stricken vehicle I found two elderly women inside, both still seat-belted in. One lady was in her 60's and the passenger must have been in her 90's. Both were conscious and speaking but bleeding from their heads. I kept them where they were and tried to reassure them, at which time an off-duty nurse also stopped to assist and she took over the immediate care of the ladies.

I went back down the road and gestured as best as I could to oncoming traffic to steer out into the other lanes, to try and avoid anyone ploughing into the back of the crashed car. Luckily being Boxing Day there was little traffic on the road. An Avon and Somerset Police officer soon arrived but was on his own, so he handed me a spare high-visibility jacket from his car and I helped him cone off the lanes. A couple of ambulances and the fire brigade soon arrived as well and tended to the casualties. From the tyre tracks it appeared that the car had driven up a steep embankment at the side of the road and rolled over its roof, back down again to where it ended up. How it had happened was up to the attending officers to work out, but when I heard from the cop a week later he let me know that both ladies had made a full recovery with only minor scratches. Ever since then I carried a police high-vis jacket in the boot of my car and it came in use on more than one occasion. This is something that I would advise all officers to do, as cops are never really off-duty and would be expected to help at any incident they come across in their daily lives. I was there for about an hour, helping the attending emergency services and using my skills, just as the off-duty nurse did as well, before continuing my journey; happy to help people who needed it, with little thought for myself on the live motorway.

***

This motorway crash was by no means the most serious RTC [Road Traffic Collision] I dealt with early in my career. I had only been on the streets about a year before one morning shift at around 08:00 a call came over the radio "anyone free to attend an immediate RTC at Canning Circus? Lorry Vs. Pedestrian". That phrase is unlikely to ever mean that the collision is minor so I jumped in with one of the blue-light trained drivers and we went to investigate.

On arrival it was immediately obvious we needed more officers, but luckily the fire and ambulance services were already on scene. The pedestrian involved had been run over and was trapped underneath the last two wheels of the trailer of a full articulated lorry. The fire service were desperately trying to jack it up with pneumatic airbags and wooden blocks. My colleague and I immediately set to work clearing onlookers and closing off roads. I requested every other available officer to attend, with the incident happening on one of the city's busiest trunk road junctions at rush hour.

Whilst the firefighters and paramedics got to work I was trying to direct where I needed other officers for road closures and think of diversion routes from a mental map of the area in my head. As I was doing this I was suddenly approached by a Superintendent 'Dave' who had been on his way into work and had been stuck in the traffic near the front of the queue. He simply came up and asked me "where do you want me?" whilst putting a high-vis police jacket on. He didn't want to take command of the situation that he obviously thought I was handling well enough, and was probably outside of his specific recent knowledge area where he'd not been at the 'sharp end' for several years in the higher ranks. Dave was another top-quality boss who was inspiring to me in my early service and who remained in touch with me throughout my career. I've been fortunate to work under several senior officers like this; but unfortunately also several the opposite.

I was directed by witnesses to the lorry driver and secured him, taking his initial verbal account. Given the severity of the crash I was requested by the Serious Collision Investigation Unit officers (those who come out and measure the skid marks and reconstruct the collisions) to take him to the police station and wait with him where a detective from their team would come and interview him. The driver was really in a bad way emotionally and was visibly shaking and in shock at what had happened.

The poor elderly gentleman who was run over did not survive, tragically passing away at the scene. It transpired from witness accounts and the investigation that the victim had got off a bus at the stop where the collision occurred. The lorry had stopped behind the bus whilst it unloaded its passengers, unable to pass. The victim had gone to the back of the bus and begun to cross the road, at which point the bus pulled off and the lorry along with it. The victim had been stood right underneath the front driver's side of the lorry cab peering out into the road to see round the lorry whether it was safe to cross. The cab was at least six feet higher than the road so the driver simply could not see him. The male had gone under the lorry cab and the trailer and the driver hadn't even realised. It was only a passer-by shouting and gesticulating at the driver that had caused him to stop, unfortunately with the poor victim still underneath the trailer wheels. The man never stood a chance, but would have died near instantly which is hopefully a small comfort to his friends and family.

This was my first real experience of multi-agency major incident working. I found that watching the fire fighters and paramedics work in these situations continued to impress me throughout my career. Their hours of training, both within their own professions and jointly with the others, all comes together to give those they are helping the best possible chance in any situation. Joint emergency services working today is the best it has ever been and there is a real 'one-team' inter-service ethos at any major incident that I have ever been to. Every agency works harmoniously together to achieve the common goal of saving lives. There is a lot of inter-service banter between the different emergency services, but all police officers, paramedics and firefighters know that when it matters they can trust each other implicitly to know exactly what needs to be done. Each knows their roles and responsibilities, give each other space and respect each other's professional judgements. Sometimes large multi-agency responses come in for criticism where they don't always get things right, but it's never through choice, and for every one time it goes wrong, there are 99 where great co-operation shines through to help those that need it.

The lorry driver was not prosecuted, after it was ascertained that he'd not been able to see the male underneath his cab at all. Still to this day I can't pass that section of road without remembering the sight of the poor man under the lorry wheels. It gives me goosebumps. This is the case for many jobs that officers, and all emergency services personnel go to. A Cambridge University study in 2018 found that **one in five** police officers experience PTSD symptoms compared to less than one in twenty of the general population. And of those that don't get outright PTSD, half of officers still reported issues with sleeping, anxiety and / or fatigue.[*] This is a very newly emerging area of research amongst the police and other emergency services which will hopefully lead into greater recognition of the sacrifices that they make on behalf of society. Since Austerity came in 2012 police have faced a real-term pay cut of some 18% according to the Police Federation, as a result of pay freezes and loss of incremental pay point salary increases. This corresponded with a reduction in staffing (officers and civilian) also of 18% in the same time period, increasing the burdens and subsequent stress on officers. Hopefully these figures around the impact that working with regular trauma has on a police officer's psyche can lead to better renumeration for officers as well as a dramatic uplift in numbers, to reduce individual exposure.

***

Other incidents are traumatic in other ways. On a works night on in 2011 we were all enjoying ourselves as a team. Work nights out were normally fairly restrained because as a group of police officers out in town, especially when you work that area, a lot of the door staff recognise you so there is a desire to avoid trouble. We were in

---

[*] Brewin, Chris *et al. Posttraumatic Stress Disorder and complex posttraumatic stress disorder in UK police officers* Cambridge University Press Online (2020) available at www.cam.ac.uk/policeptsd

one of the city's many bars when a colleague of mine accidentally knocked into a man and spilt his drink. Hastily apologising, my colleague offered to buy him another one, but before he could even get his words out the male smashed a glass bottle into his face, slicing it open all down one cheek, and fled the scene. My colleague is genuinely one of the nicest people you could ever meet and the type of officer you would want attending if your gran was burgled. He spent days in intensive care having reconstructive surgery. He returned to work a few months later and is still an officer to this day, but bears a large scar on his face from that night. The offender was caught after an excellent investigation by the CID and sent to prison for several years. There was no indication that the offender knew that my colleague was a police officer, it was just a completely random act of violence unfortunately typical of any city centre weekend across the country. The incident really brought home the reality that each and every victim of crime is someone's family, friend or colleague, and served as a reminder that there are just plain nasty, violent people out there, who will cause horrific injury without a second thought.

***

Dealing with traumatic incidents is fairly routine to a degree for a front-line response police officer and I certainly got my fair share of violent crimes during my probationary period. One night shift I was out with the Sergeant when a request came over the radio to attend reports from the ambulance service of a young man reporting he'd been shot. In these situations the ambulance service will pass it straight to the police to attend and assess whether there is any remaining threat in the area before their crews attend to the casualty. When we found the victim, as is so often the case with these types of incidents, he didn't want to tell us anything about what had happened. He showed us the wound in his leg, which for a gunshot wound compared to what you see on TV was fairly anti-climactic. There was a small puncture wound in his leg with no exit wound and it indeed turned out from x-rays that the low calibre bullet had hit his femur and lodged in his leg. This chap wasn't even the intended target and had simply been out walking with his friend who was, but it still didn't mean he wanted to help the police with their enquiries to locate the person responsible.

This is so often the case with victims of stabbings and shootings, who do not want to co-operate with the police. This can be for a variety of reasons which can include:

- Not wanting to be seen as a grass,
- Having been brought up in an environment where they are taught not to speak to the police
- some kind of misplaced sense of bravado that they are too big or too 'hard' to need any help,
- and some kind of sense of intent to sort it out themselves.

The truth is most likely a collection of all or some of the above. The odds of being an entirely innocent victim of a stabbing or shooting are quite slim (but they do happen unfortunately) and it is the duty of the police to investigate these types of serious offences even when the victim doesn't want to co-operate. This wasn't always the case – even a decade or so previously it would have simply been seen as 'baddie-on-baddie' and just written off. The potential of future harm to society from these kinds of incidents is thankfully now recognised and they are investigated regardless of victim co-operation. They take up masses of police time however, from the initial response from uniformed officers standing on crime scenes and potentially encountering the armed offender to the CID teams who conduct the investigation. They also give the city of Nottingham a really bad reputation, such as it received in the early 2000's earning the nickname 'Shottingham'. To make it worse, most of these incidents occur over some trivial perceived 'insult' or 'disrespect' of one group (or gang) to another or even petty fall-outs between individuals. I have known shootings that have happened between teenagers following a fall-out over a girl or lyrics 'dissing' another gang in a song.

Another act of extreme but meaningless violence happened on an afternoon when police were called to a street in Radford. A drunken argument between housemates had turned violent and ended up with one attacking the other with an axe. When we got there the victim had a large chunk cut out of his head. He was somehow still alive and trying to speak but not making a great deal of sense and the noise he was making was awful, a kind of rattling groan. Where the axe had cut away part of his head his brain was visible. A colleague arrested the offender who was still in the house, and another travelled to the hospital with the victim whilst I remained at the address to preserve the scene for forensics officers. The sight of a man with a good portion of the side of his head missing is not something that leaves you. I believe that the victim from this lived (I don't remember a murder investigation following), although as with so many other incidents that go to different departments (CID) to investigate I never did find out the outcome for the victim or suspect.

'Preserving crime scenes' and escorting detained persons from custody to hospitals takes up an inordinate amount of time of uniformed officers. The need to ensure the integrity of crime scenes for the avoidance of accusations of post-incident tampering when cases get to court is obvious, and this requirement has existed for decades in policing. It does unfortunately take up a lot for time of uniformed officers and can leave the response teams very short-staffed overnight when there are no other teams on duty. During the day they are often covered by PCSO's or neighbourhood 'beat managers.

What has got significantly worse in recent years is the frequency of taking arrested persons to hospital. Word seems to have filtered out to the criminal fraternity around what they need to allege to custody staff in order to go to hospital. Whilst most 'normal-minded' folk may find the idea of a four-hour wait in a hospital A&E department nightmarish, it's infinitely more preferable to being sat in a police cell for the same time. The police service nationally are (fairly justifiably) terrified of the prospect of having a death in custody, so the 'frequent flyers' will often claim any number of ailments from the following which guarantees them a trip to hospital:

- Swallowing drugs immediately prior to arrest (often in spite of police officers having been with them for some time before going to custody)
- Head injuries
- Heart palpitations
- Shortness of breath
- Some who have ongoing ailments such as broken limbs, chronic skin conditions or similar, will intentionally not seek hospital treatment themselves and instead wait until they are arrested so that the police have to take them and they can avoid waiting in the cells.

This escort duty takes up a minimum of two officers for the duration of the period that the person is at the hospital and if they are violent it can sometimes take more. If the person is particularly vile they will spend the entire time at hospital shouting profanities and being abusive to anyone and everyone there. This is awful for public perception as all the ill people in the waiting area look to you to stop your prisoner from being abusive, but they're already under arrest and you can't simply take them back to custody as the staff there will turn you around and send you back to hospital unless the detainee has been seen by the medical staff. The hospital don't fast-track persons in custody just to free up police time. If you were ill and had been waiting two hours to see a doctor, would you want an alleged criminal to cut the line in front of you? Often the doctor's tactic to diagnose and treat the supposed issues of arrested people is to simply let them wait six hours by which time any issue they claim to be afflicted with would have manifested itself. For young-in-service officers (who won't have additional skills such as blue-light driving, Taser, 'riot' training or anything else that makes them slightly more valuable to be available,) many long shifts are spent either guarding a crime scene or sat with someone at hospital.

On one such occasion of 'babysitting' someone at hospital in my early career, I was sat with a different shooting victim at the Queen's Medical Centre Hospital. This had the dual function of both protecting him from any outstanding suspects and to let detectives know when he regained consciousness so they could speak to him. Quite what I would have done as an unarmed officer if some armed offenders had turned up wanting to finish the job I don't know! It always makes me laugh on police TV dramas when victims are guarded at hospital by an armed officer – I've never known it happen. The victim had been shot in the head with a shotgun and when I arrived he had been taken into surgery to have the pellets removed. I waited in the recovery room for him to be brought out and when he was, the doctors brought out a little medical pot full of small round lead pellets that they had removed from his head, handing this to me to seize as evidence.

It always appears the case that those involved in criminality seem to survive horrific encounters. It is most apparent in car crashes following pursuits or dangerous driving, where the person responsible will crash into an innocent member of the public and walk away from it completely unscathed. The poor people that they crash into who were simply going about their legitimate business though invariably suffer life changing injuries or death. It's the same with stabbings and shootings. Those who are known criminals often survive being shot or stabbed, but the innocent victims who fall foul of these types of incidents seem far more likely to die. This is probably just because those incidents where the victims are innocents stick in the memory more, but ask any police officer and they will tell you the same. Criminals by-and-large are also thankfully fairly incompetent at actually inflicting serious harm on one another such as in this case, although obviously that's not always true. Perhaps this explains why all the bad guys in Hollywood movies can never shoot well?

This wasn't even the worst surgical experience during my early service. That came one time when a colleague and I were sent to watch a prisoner who had been arrested overnight for glassing someone. In doing so, the suspect had got a large strand of glass embedded along the length of his thumb. X-rays had shown the surgeons that the only way to remove the glass safely was to partially amputate the thumb and pull the glass out, then stitch the thumb back on. This didn't require a full anaesthetic, only a local one to the hand, which in turn meant that throughout the procedure our detainee would be conscious and able to move all his body bar his hand.

A quick chat with the surgical staff confirmed that there were two entrances to the operating theatre, so it was not possible to simply wait outside whilst they did the procedure. One of us had to go in. A quick pulling of seniority by my partner who had more service than me and the deal was settled. I had to go into the operating theatre with the suspect whilst he had his thumb all but chopped off. I was required to wear a full surgical gown, hair net and boot covers, as well as scrub all my hands and arms to be as clean as possible. I was then shown to a seat in the corner of the room where I had to at least keep a partial view of the suspect. I'm generally not squeamish and had already seen some pretty horrific things by this time in my career, but as the surgery got underway this proved to not be the case.

Whether it was the hospital setting and the clinical sterile smell or something else, but when they had sawn through most of the thumb at the joint and essentially folded it backwards so the thumbnail was touching the base of the thumb, I could feel myself feeling lighter and lighter-headed. I was taking noticeably quicker breaths and everything went a bit blurry. I couldn't help but start hunching over and not looking at the surgery or prisoner. This still didn't help as I could see it in my mind's-eye. Luckily one of the nurses obviously saw my struggles, remarked on how pale I looked and got me a cup of water. This helped a bit as well as taking some time to get my breathing under control, by which time thankfully they were nearly finished.

I'm forever grateful that I was sat behind the prisoner so he couldn't see me, because if he had got up and left at that point there wasn't a whole lot I could have done to stop him – short of dramatically falling to the floor in a faint! The sole redeeming feature of this situation was that barring the operating theatre staff, none of my colleagues were around to witness my discomfort. Had any of them found about this (before now!) then I would have no doubt owed a 'cake fine'. This is how minor errors or transgressions are dealt with generally in the police service. The 'offender' is required by their team to bring cakes in by way of an apology (or celebration of a good achievement). Nearly fainting at the sight of minor surgery would have almost certainly constituted a 'cake offence' as do other small infractions such being a few minutes late for work; forgetting your warrant card at home; or making an error on paperwork to name but a few examples. As so much of police work revolves around different laws stemming from Acts of Parliament, some enterprising officers somewhere created a 'Cake Offences Act', which if you search on Google will provide a comprehensive list of all things that can earn cake fines. Some teams I worked on I probably gained several pounds as a result of the slip-ups of colleagues!

(I feel it necessary to clarify that the Cake Offences Act only applies for light-hearted transgressions or mishaps. Actual larger-scale errors are reported and investigated appropriately by the PSD or suitable person.)

***

A lot of the time police officers deal with the aftermath of traumatic incidents, but very rarely do they witness them in person. With the increase in the coverage of CCTV, the control room operators do occasionally see some quite horrifying things, and you can tell as an officer on the ground when something is serious from the dispatchers' reactions.

I was on a 'Night Time Economy' shift in the city centre one weekend, policing the night time revellers in company with my Sergeant at the time. We were on foot on Theatre Square when a request came over the radio for officers to attend King Street for a couple of males squaring up to each other. As we weren't far away we offered to go. On-route we continued receiving updates from our dispatcher, who was regularly on our radio channel and normally quite unflappable. We were told that punches were being thrown and quickened our pace to get there, even more so when we were told that one male had been punched to the floor. The next updates were almost unheard of for normally very professional radio interactions, where everyone knows that all the communications are recorded and can be used in evidence. They went as follows:

Operator: "One male is now on the floor, and the other two are kicking him, they're.... *Oh, shit.*"

When you hear that on the radio you know something bad has happened and sure enough we were told that one of the males had jumped off the pavement onto the head of the victim laying on the floor. This is an horrific act and can easily lead to death. After this update my Sergeant and I were at full sprint, by now turning onto King Street and were being given descriptions of the two males. They clearly glimpsed two fast-moving hi-vis jackets heading their way and decided to run the opposite direction. We chased them and the Sergeant managed to detain one by running full pelt into him, slamming him into a wall and arresting him. I went after the other who had a bit more of a head-start and chased him for several streets, shouting each new location into the radio as I ran. There is little more exhilarating than a foot chase, as your adrenaline soars, you start breathing heavily and your vision largely focuses down onto the subject you're chasing. It's an almost primeval act – chasing down your fleeing 'prey'. I could hear the great sound of the sirens of police cars converging on me from across the city as I gained on the chap. As he saw his path blocked by an arriving police car he stopped and held his hands up, allowing me to grab him and put handcuffs on him – ensuring the fists he'd been using so ruthlessly on another human only moments ago were neutralised. Both males were arrested for Wounding with Intent (a.k.a GBH) and I believe received reasonable custodial sentences, thanks largely to the CCTV.

My Sergeant and I got several e-mails from the control room staff over the next few days saying they'd watched us detain the offenders on CCTV and described my Sergeant's arrest as like something off 'The Sweeney'! The suspect wasn't hurt during the arrest and what is often not understood by the public who have never done policing, is that it's sometimes necessary to go in at a high level of force in order to ensure no-one else (or you) is injured by someone who's clearly not afraid to cause serious violence. Simply walking over to such an aggressive individual, more than likely under the influence of drink and/or drugs and asking politely if they'd mind going with you to the police station is unlikely to cut it and not a risk worth taking. This is often what gets forgotten by certain sectors of society who frequently claim that police use excessive force. Until you have tried detaining someone 'off their face' on cocaine or amphetamines and realise that it can take six or more people of a similar size to that person to even hope to achieve it, you are ill-equipped to judge on levels of force.

I've seen reports and videos of members of civil liberties organisations in America going on police firearms training courses. When they're suddenly exposed to the intense pressure of making split-second decisions they invariably end up 'shooting' innocent people in the training exercises. I am a strong advocate that those who cry 'police brutality' should come on ride-alongs with police officers and witness the level of violence offered to them. Whilst present at volatile situations they could offer alternative solutions to how they might be able to better deal with violent individuals who through substance abuse or mental health issues cannot be reasoned with. I don't imagine they'd be very successful, but it would be the officers they were with who would step in to protect them.

***

Perhaps the most serious and sustained violent incident I was ever involved in occurred during my probationary period when I helped to deal with the riots of 2011. In London on 4th August 2011 the Metropolitan Police shot and killed known gang member Mark Duggan. An intelligence-led operation identified that he had been seen to purchase and be in possession of a firearm. What followed is well documented and was experienced by cities across the country, Nottingham included.

The night of the shooting saw rioting break out in London and this spread to Nottingham the following night. I was on my last day off and was due to be on a day shift the following morning. As the evening went on, the news and social media revealed more and more coverage of riots in Nottingham. Shops were hastily boarding their windows and there were pictures of a large-scale police deployment in the city including officers in full riot gear and the force's now defunct mounted team outside the Victoria shopping centre. Late in the evening Canning Circus Police Station was subject to a firebomb attack when a large group of hooded youths with their faces covered, surrounded it and threw home-made petrol bombs at the building. They succeeded in setting light to the canopy outside the main door before being chased away by a police dog and a couple of very brave local response officers. Officers inside the police station managed to put the fire out with an extinguisher.

It was probably one of the most difficult decisions I had to make early in my career, when I knew I was due in early the following morning but I could see in the news that additional officers were desperately needed on duty there and then. I ultimately concluded that I would be needed the following day to help deal with any arrested persons or scenes that needed securing and to continue providing a policing response to anyone else who needed it. I went to bed late and got up early to go in and let the night shift go home after what had no doubt been a very busy tour of duty.

The bosses quickly realised that my control room experience meant that I knew my way around all the command-and-control systems as well as having relevant training and experience in multi-agency co-operation and resource deployment. I was seconded into the 'gold command' suite to work alongside representatives from the fire brigade, ambulance service, council, housing and emergency planning. From in there I helped the senior officers by acting as liaison to these other agencies, as well as monitoring police command-and-control systems for any incidents that may be linked to disorder. I was also tasked to share information on any property destruction or issues that any of the partner agencies would need to be aware of. It was a fascinating role that allowed me to see the decision-making processes of the senior officers present. I ended up working a long shift that day until late at night when it became apparent that after the first night the rioters had either given up or realised that they wouldn't be able to loot businesses or attack the police in Nottingham. This was due almost entirely to the swift and decisive response from the police here, which was widely praised in comparison to the response from some other areas.

I thought I'd had a gruelling day, but it became folk-lore in the force that the DCI in charge of the subsequent investigation worked some 72 hours straight, ensuring everyone arrested was processed in line with legislation and put before the court as promptly as possible. Dozens of people were charged and remanded into custody for serious offences and the sentences handed out by the courts were exemplary; including one more silly individual who had taken pictures of his home-made firebombs in his shower and sent them to all his friends from his phone. That evidence was fairly conclusive when showed to the court...

There was a period of a couple of years where the local prisons were rather full; and then slowly but surely a few years after that it would be a regular occurrence to check someone against the Police National Computer and be informed they had "recent previous for rioting". It was primarily our 'regular customers' who were involved and who clearly weren't protesting about what had happened in London, but instead saw it as an opportunity to loot sports and electronics shops (the Waterstones book shop in town was one of the only ones to not even board its windows!) to try and steal goods, as well as to attack the police and believe that they could be anonymous in the crowd. Unfortunately for them Nottingham is not a large city and most of them were identified from CCTV footage and prosecuted.

The riots were to give me a fantastic insight into the intricacies of multi-agency working and collaboration both between local partners and police forces nationally. Other officers came to Nottingham for a period of several days after this first night from neighbouring local forces that hadn't experienced any disorder. The united 'can-do' attitude of all the agencies involved in the hastily established joint control room demonstrated to me the spirit of service from a whole range of public bodies. Everyone was there to try and prevent as much damage or disorder as their role allowed them and to put right any issues as soon as practicable. It was reminiscent of the behaviours shown by the different emergency services at the fatal traffic collision, but was more surprising given how rarely city-wide critical incidents such as the riots occur.

***

It became clear to me early on in my career how significantly TV and film influence people's reactions and how they feel they should behave when confronted by the police. It's something that I found quite funny whenever I actually thought about it. One example would be the case covered earlier where the offender stamped on the victim's head, and how when I caught him, he felt compelled to put his hands up in the air. This is not an uncommon reaction for people when they're caught by the police. British police aren't routinely armed, but it's that common on films and television that maybe that's what some people feel they're expected to do.

Perhaps the best time that film had influenced someone's actions was one of the first times I needed to use force at an incident. I'd gone with my tutor to assist another colleague arresting a male who was known to have previously been violent. When James and I arrived, our colleague told the man that he was being arrested and his genuine reply was "You'll never take me alive, coppers"! I had a moment where I honestly wondered what I'd signed up for and if the TV shows were actually real. Needless to say he did come to custody alive and well. Sadly no-one since has ever said this to me again and policing definitely turned out not to be what you see on the telly.

Other incidents are similarly humorous for various reasons. When I was still young in service one of my team members was a former elite armed forces soldier and was one of the fittest people I've ever encountered. He rarely if ever wore body armour and it was often jokingly suggested that if he was shot, the bullets would bounce off him anyway! One evening we were on duty when a call came over the radio to reports of youths breaking into a business premises in the city. By good fortune this officer was just round the corner from it and was on scene within minutes.

Sure enough the arrival of the blue lights outside prompted three offenders to run out of the building they were burgling, hotly pursued by the officer. As the rest of us were all still driving to the scene the radio traffic we heard was as follows:

Officer: "On scene. Got three runners down the street. [descriptions].

"I've caught one, handcuffed him to a lamppost on this street, going after the other two if someone can get to him.

"Got a second, he's handcuffed to some railings on the next street if someone can go to him as well."

"Control, can I have someone to me as well please on the hurry-up, I've currently got the third one pinned to the floor just up from the other one but haven't got any other cuffs."

I didn't witness this impressive foot chase with my own eyes, but when I remember that radio traffic I have an image of the T-1000 from 'Terminator 2'. I'm not sure that handcuffing people to railings or lampposts is an approved trained technique, but policing is sometimes about improvisation, and three suspects were brought to justice thanks to the impressive fitness and abilities of this officer.

***

Mental health conditions also play a part in occasionally providing humorous situations – obviously not at the time when someone is clearly struggling with genuine medical issues – but in hindsight by appearing somewhat surreal. I attended an incident with a colleague near to Nottingham Castle where someone had heard noises coming from a wooded area on the side of the cliff. For quite a while we couldn't see or hear anything and were about to leave when a male voice began shouting that he was our "lord and saviour" and that we were "trespassing on sacred ground". We tried to speak to the disembodied voice but couldn't see where it was coming from due to it being dark and him being hidden in the trees. From speaking to him it was clear he was suffering from an acute mental health crisis, which made negotiating him down quite difficult. What made it even more challenging was that as we were trying to coax him down he began throwing items at us. These were the most random assortment of items that it would be possible to conceive of, and as they came hurtling out the darkness at us, all were accompanied by some form of explanation of their religious link to the man throwing them. Items included a hollow brass orb that was apparently a holy relic and a sandal that was the shoe worn on a holy pilgrimage.

We were stood dodging occasional missiles and listening to the abuse directed at us for a few hours as we tried to negotiate, unable to climb the steep cliff face to a man who held the high ground and who had demonstrated he wasn't concerned about throwing things at us. Eventually we formed a plan to appear to leave but actually hide and then return ten minutes later to see if the male got bored without a captive audience. Sure enough this worked perfectly and as we hid from view we heard a rustling noise as a figure dressed in dirty tatty clothes emerged from the undergrowth. We promptly grabbed the man who was ultimately quite compliant and detained him under the Mental Health Act, taking him to a place of safety where he could be assessed and receive suitable treatment.

It was during this incident on a cold winter's evening, having various objects appear out of the darkness hurtling towards me, that I experienced my first adrenaline dump of my career. I began shivering uncontrollably and couldn't stop myself. It was a shivering that was not a result of the cold and was not borne out of overwhelming fear. I remember distinctly not being afraid, more just confused by the whole situation, but with underlying concern in case one of the more solid objects being thrown did hit me. For whatever reason, probably a combination of the cold and the protracted uncertainty, this adrenaline dump occurred. I would guess at the shivering being a result of the cold and the adrenaline wearing off after having been there such a long time.

This was not the only time in my career I was to experience this similar feeling of uncontrollable shivering but being the first I didn't really understand it. I remember that every time it happened I was acutely conscious of anyone seeing the uncontrollable shaking and unsteadiness of my hands, finding it quite embarrassing. This was especially the case when it occurred later in my career in situations where I was dealing with some quite nasty individuals, who look to prey on any weakness shown by officers stopping them. I have no idea if this has or does happen to any other officers and how they react to it, but I can't imagine that I was alone with this. There was no pattern or predictability around when it occurred and it was not a common occurrence, but happened often enough to be something that would always be in the back of my mind when dealing with anything that had a potential to escalate.

***

An incident at the end of my probationary period provided humour of a different kind, mostly due to the stupidity and sheer brazenness of the suspect, but simultaneously provided some real job satisfaction in being able to help lots of victims. It also kick-started my long relationship with the force communications team and made me realise the benefits of positive news for the force, especially at a time before individual officers could put such events on social media.

It was late December 2011 when I got sent to a parcel distribution warehouse for an incident that one of the delivery couriers had reported to his manager, saying that he'd been robbed on his round "by a bunch of gypsies". I arrived at the depot and spoke to the supposed victim, who told me that he had been doing his delivery round when he was overtaken by a car that suddenly stopped in front of him. Several men got out with weapons and balaclavas on and threatened him, before emptying the contents of the back of his van and taking his sat nav. Given the time of year, the stolen items were likely to all be Christmas presents which made the robbery particularly heinous. The driver was reasonably credible and the circumstances, although far-fetched, weren't outside the realms of possibility. There was something not quite right about the chap's account though, which was really specific in some parts but really vague in others. After speaking to him I went to have a word in private with his supervisor who was also present and had heard the driver's account.

I asked him whether the driver's account had been the same to him and he said it had been, but we both couldn't understand why the driver had driven all the way back to the depot to report the matter rather than from the scene, and he also didn't seem that shaken. He said the driver was agency staff who had only been taken on a few weeks before as part of the Christmas period uplift so he didn't really know him. Something about the whole situation wasn't right though and my 'copper's nose' (definitely a real thing that officers get with experience in the job – a real sense for when people are lying or something isn't quite right) was most definitely tingling. I ran it by my Sergeant, who was very trusting of me and agreed that if I felt it was off to proceed with what I thought best. The course of action I felt best was to arrest the driver (the supposed victim) for theft, as I firmly suspected that he had taken the goods. I went back to the driver and said the immortal words and his reaction to being arrested told me all I needed to know about the truth of the matter. There was no resistance at all, no denials, just an apparent reluctant acceptance of his fate.

After booking someone into custody police officers can get an authority to search the arrested person's address. I got the paperwork signed and together with the Sergeant travelled to the suspect's home which was a rented farmhouse with a barn outside. Knocking on the door we could see a woman inside who had blatantly heard and seen us but was not answering the door. In perhaps the most damning indication we were on the right track, we could see through the window that she was hurriedly piling items into a cupboard! Eventually after we made it clear that we would be forcing entry, she opened the door. We went in, explained our powers and why we were there and then walked into the living room where we had seen her through the window. In that room we discovered several cellophane wrapped boxes containing assorted brands of laptops; sealed postage bags from various online clothing retailers; and other sealed cardboard boxes with addresses on, none of which were for the premises we were at, but *were* in the area the courier was supposed to be delivering to...

We immediately arrested the female for handling stolen goods and crucially as we continued looking, we found a sat nav in the house as well. We plugged this into the power socket in our police car and very helpfully the last journey programmed into the device was from a location on the delivery route of the male we had arrested back to his home address! Further searches outside in the barn and a horse box trailer yielded numerous other packages. Clearly realising by this point that the game was up, the woman at the address had helped us to locate these extra packages outside. We took her into custody and booked the parcels into police property. The man was later charged with theft and perverting the course of justice and the woman was issued a caution for handling stolen goods. His theft was motivated entirely by greed and we found out that the pair were living well beyond their means and were stealing the items to sell on in order to fund their lavish lifestyles.

The following day I came to work early and returned all the seized items to the delivery depot, ensuring with the manager I had spoken to the previous day that they would be delivered ASAP and still in time for Christmas. Recognising the value of the positive news story I contacted the force communications team who put out a press release in the local paper about the 'Cop who Saved Christmas'. I was also interviewed by BBC Radio Nottingham – a very embarrassing interview in which I declared that it "gave me a warm fuzzy feeling inside" helping ensure people didn't miss out! This was the first time I gave an interview with the media or had a story about me in the paper, but it certainly wasn't to be the last.

***

In an example of some even more stupid offenders occurred during my time as a special constable, in an incident that also gave me a brush with a 'celebrity'. A key function of the special constabulary is providing policing support at larger events by enabling a uniformed law enforcement presence, but maintaining staffing levels of officers on 'normal' duties. To this end specials are regularly requested to provide staffing for events such as the Nottingham marathon, various parades and music festivals. I often used to volunteer for these events as they would not only be great fun but also relatively easy to work – it was mostly just ensuring road closures were adhered to and providing a visible presence. Some events were particularly good to work. I once watched Nottingham legend Carl 'The Cobra' Froch fight at the Nottingham Arena without having to pay a penny because I was working it as a special. I also regularly worked the city's Splendour music festival which allowed me to provide excellent community relations with the families that attended, as well as watch the music for free!

It was whilst working the Splendour festival one year that I had repeated encounters with a pair of drunken idiots who were continually trying to 'jump the fence' and get in without paying. They'd been caught each time by security, and after their second or third attempt the security guards had flagged down a colleague and me to take more formal action. Whilst they hadn't committed any criminal offences, only a civil matter of trying to get in without paying, we gave them strong words of advice regarding any further issues being likely to result in them being arrested for being drunk and disorderly. About half an hour later the same security guard from before came over to us on our fixed point and said that there was trouble in the artists' tour bus parking area. He beckoned us there quite quickly and after a short jog we arrived to see the same drunken pair kicking at a door of one of the tour buses. We ran over but they saw us before we got close and 'gave it legs'. Unfortunately those legs weren't that steady as a result of all their drink and my colleague managed to get one after barely a few steps, pinning him up against the tour bus. The second one continued running for a short distance but the combination of drink and the loose gravel meant that he slipped over as he tried to round a corner. I was on him like a flash, only then realising that he was built like the proverbial outhouse. I needn't have worried though because no sooner was I on him than the security guard piled in as well, who was even more muscular than the suspect!

A short scrap ensued between the three of us but the handcuffs went on fairly quickly and I arrested him for being drunk and disorderly. The other buffoon was already in cuffs when we got back to my colleague, and we had a police transport van take us to the custody suite. It was only when we arrived there that we had time to actually check the pair on police computers. The result came back that the chap I'd arrested was already wanted for questioning on suspicion of a serious assault alleged to have occurred several months previously, where he'd been accused of fracturing another man's skull. My prisoner was essentially on the run from justice trying to avoid facing into the consequences of this previous allegation. I further arrested him for that offence and passed the case on to CID who were very grateful.

Also very grateful was Kate Nash, the singer who was headlining the festival that year and whose tour bus the pair had been trying to get into whilst she was inside. She was already on stage by the time my colleague and I returned to the site, but the security guard passed on a message from her that she was incredibly thankful for our swift and decisive actions. The male I arrested received a couple of years' imprisonment for the serious assault and was only caught because his drunken stupidity and determination to get into the very reasonably priced festival for free attracted police attention. You can't help some people. It's often said that but for drugs and alcohol, the police would be mostly out of work and that certainly rings true to me.

Developing My Skills

Running the Queen off her own Highway...

I stayed on response for another three years after completing my two-year probationary period, remaining covering the City Centre, Radford and Lenton areas of Nottingham. During this time I was based initially at Central Police Station on North Church Street, then moved to the Riverside Police Station just outside The Meadows, and finally to Radford Road Police Station. This quick succession of police stations within a three-year period was as a result of the station closures and force restructures as a result of Austerity measures.

I loved working the 'Canning Circus Neighbourhood Policing Area' throughout my career. It comprised an eclectic mix of inner-city working-class families in tight terraced housing in Lenton Abbey, contrasting with the affluent mansions on the   gas-lit avenues of The Park Estate; large families heavily reliant on benefits living cheek-by-jowl in the Lenton area with cash-rich students who have few cares in the world; diverse cultures from across Europe, Africa and Asia who sometimes speak little English in the Radford area bordering areas comprising predominantly white middle-class suburbanites such as Wollaton. The mix of incidents and people was probably more varied than any other Neighbourhood Policing Area in the city and probably the whole county. This variety really helped keep the job interesting for me.

Completing my response driving course (blue lights) shortly after the conclusion of my probation gave me a new degree of freedom and the ability to attend more incidents. My enthusiasm and passion for the job meant that I attended as many calls as possible. I would often be off work late due to dealing with a prisoner or sorting out paperwork from the last-minute incident that I volunteered to attend just before the next team started. I was young and had no real commitments at home so I enjoyed the work, the overtime money and really felt that I was supporting the older officers who had children to get home to.

I hadn't long completed my two-year probation when planning for the Olympics was reaching its final stages and the policing commitments were beginning to be known. Not wanting to miss the opportunity to be part of this 'once-in-a-lifetime' spectacle I volunteered for a stint in London. There were two requirements of Nottinghamshire Police. One was a four-day commitment in the run-up to the Olympics to ensure the 'hard search' of the perimeter (for bombs, weapons caches etc), once completed by specialist search teams, could be preserved; and the other was for a 21 day deployment covering the entire period of the Olympics. I landed the four-day attachment but wasn't disappointed because it still meant I would get to be part of something great. As it was, the four-day period felt like 21, as we worked an average of 18 hours each day. I use the term 'worked' very loosely as whilst we were on duty for 18 hours, a large part of both days was spent sat around waiting for deployment or being transported to our areas.

The first day was spent travelling to London from Nottingham and getting ourselves set up in the student halls of residence in Hertford that had been taken over by the police as a personnel base. That day was not taxing and we enjoyed a few drinks in the bar that night, but had an 08:00 hours start the following morning for our deployment to the Olympic Park. We rendezvoused at the required time the following morning but there was no coach to meet us. After our Inspector made some phone enquiries we were stood down and re-convened at 11:00. We boarded the coach that took us to the forward deployment centre on the outskirts of London, which was a fancy name for a large marquee and coach park in a gravel car park. There we were given lunch and told we would be deployed at 14:00 to be on the ground for 15:00.

At 18:00 after numerous false alarms and having just been sat around in our full uniforms for some six hours now in blazing heat, we were finally called onto a coach. And what a coach it was! Presumably due to it being football off-season, or the massive number of coaches required for transporting all the Olympics personnel, the coach that arrived to transport us to the Olympic Park was the Southampton FC team coach! Riding in this leather-seated, air-conditioned, mini-fridge bedecked luxury was extravagant indeed and none of us really felt like getting off at the other end. After we de-bussed and our Inspector liaised with his counterpart who we were taking off, we established that we should have been on the ground at 15:00 hours to relieve the previous team of officers, as they'd been there since 07:00 hours. Suitable apologies were given and we were then deployed to walk around the outskirts of the Olympic Park – but not into it – until around midnight when we were relieved by the night shift.

During the patrols we got to watch practice runs of the 'Queen's helicopter parachute jump' stunt which was performed in the Olympic opening ceremony. Several helicopters kept coming and hovering overhead with people parachuting out of them. This caused much speculation amongst us all about what was going on, as we hadn't received any kind of briefing it was due to happen. For all we knew it was terrorists parachuting into the stadium! Inside the Park wasn't our patrol area though and nothing came over our radios requesting our assistance, so we carried on our patrols, watching them as they arrived and practiced. Sadly none of the parachutists that I could see appeared to be Daniel Craig... There were also large fireworks being set off sporadically, presumably to test timings and as a rehearsal for the following night's big event. It was about 02:30 before we arrived back at the student village and got back to bed.

The next day we were due to provide security for the pre-Olympics concert in Hyde Park which was headlined by Dizzee Rascal and others. Security for the inside of the concert was provided by the event organisers, and our duty was again to patrol the perimeter and the surrounding park, ensuring no-one jumped the fence and being a deterrent to would-be criminals. This deployment was much more successfully organised and we got to the area at around 16:00 to patrol until midnight.

It was during this deployment that the stark contrast between rural police forces and the Metropolitan Police Force was demonstrated, which was commented on by senior Met officers in their feedback to us the following day. Officers from Nottinghamshire and a couple of other regional forces patrolled in pairs, wandering around the park in their designated patrol areas, speaking to the public, having photos and generally providing reassurance as well as constant vigilance. The Met Officers in contrast, on every occasion we saw them, were stood around in large circles of a dozen or so all facing inwards and chatting with one-another. The feedback from the Met Commander in charge of the event went along the lines of them saying that they wished all their officers were more like those from the rural forces because the public feedback from the friendly presence and community engagement was overwhelmingly positive. The Commander commented on the same issue around Metropolitan Police officers being stood in huddles whereas the rural forces officers had been approachable due to only being in pairs. The event went off without a hitch and the following day we left to come back to Nottingham –

the day of the opening ceremony which I was at home to watch on the TV.

***

The Olympics was not the only celebration taking place that year, as also 2012 marked Her Royal Highness Queen Elizabeth II's Diamond Jubilee, in which she undertook a tour of the country, including visiting Nottingham. Additional police officers were deployed in numbers, but my team were on a day shift anyway. We briefed on as normal but had quite a dull morning, as the number of officers walking round the city prevented many of the normal calls we would expect.

Her Majesty The Queen greeted the crowds from the Council House balcony some time around midday. I was not fortunate enough to see this as we'd been instructed to steer clear of the area due to the numbers of other officers present. At around that time a call came over the police radio that a shoplifter had been detained who was kicking off and struggling with security. I was nearby so volunteered for the job and began blue-lighting to the location.

I was using my blue lights and sirens to carve my way through the many buses and taxis on Milton Street towards Parliament Street. All the while, unbeknownst to me, The Queen had finished greeting the crowds and had left the Council House on her way to her next engagement. Suddenly as one bus moved out the way for me, I was confronted by a large convoy of unmarked Range Rovers and Jaguars with blue lights on, heading at high speed straight towards me in the opposite direction! I instantly realised that this could mean only one thing. I quickly pulled in to the side of the road just in time to allow the fleet of high-performance cars to hurtle past me. It could only have been the convoy containing Her Majesty The Queen that I'd nearly run off the road! I dread to think the amount of 'cake fines' I would have had to pay to all my colleagues, not to mention the national news coverage, if I had run the Queen off her own Highway...

***

2012 also marked a significant year for policing and the country at large in yet another way as Austerity came to the fore. It was announced that police budgets were going to be cut by 20%, alongside pay and increment freezes and pension changes. This prompted the biggest demonstration by police officers in a generation and on 10th May 2012 I was in London again – this time off duty, but marching with 30,000 colleagues from across the country in protest at the planned cuts. This event showed how protest demonstrations can be held respectfully and with little fuss, as the 30,000 of us marched along the pre-planned route agreed by the Metropolitan Police, chanting and singing. Once the march was complete, we all dispersed with no violence, damage or other anti-social behaviour to be seen. Other protest marches could learn a lot from how the police officers carried themselves that day. This exemplary behaviour was recognised by our on-duty Metropolitan Police colleagues who were manning road closures or had come in duty time to show their support, who stood and applauded us the entire time the procession passed them.

The day was one of great pride, considering that nationally there were at that time in the region of 135,000 officers. If it's factored in that on a Thursday afternoon outside of school holidays at least half or possibly even up to two-thirds of the officers nationally had to be at work, to have had 30,000 there on the day represented the majority of those who were not on duty nationally attending. This demonstrated the strength of feeling about what was being faced by the service.

Sadly the march made little to no difference as the Home Secretary of the time, Theresa May, seemed to have a personal vendetta against the police and refused to listen to any opinions regarding the damage the cuts and reforms could bring. 20% budget cuts from a service where some 85% of costs are on wages inevitably meant that there would be a significant drop in police officer and staff numbers. This would in turn have a drastic effect on crime figures as the 'niceties' of policing that are not essentials would be the first to go – primarily community policing.

Theresa May famously accused the Police Federation of "crying wolf" in a speech she gave to the organisation's conference in 2015. The "scaremongering" was proven correct however on a local and national level. From my own personal experience, when I started as a neighbourhood beat manager in 2014 there were a team of some 12 officers and about 18 PCSO's. When I left that role only two-and-a-half years later there were just 6 officers and only 8 PCSO's remaining, following a round of redundancies and enforced retirements. Even the station we had been based at in the heart of the community had been closed down to save money. When I started my career on response in 2009 I briefed on shift with some 20 or more colleagues covering just the city centre. When I left in 2020 the city centre was lucky if it was covered by just 6 response officers. The same was true at Radford Road which went from around a dozen officers to sometimes me briefing on a team of 4. At night between 22:00 and 07:00 when most the neighbourhood and specialist teams are off duty, there can now be as few as 30 officers covering the whole of the city of Nottingham, with 6 armed response officers to call on for back-up.

At a national level the swathing cuts to front-line officer numbers saw rising crime figures, especially for knife crime. This rise in stabbings was almost certainly as a result of a rise in drug-dealing and gang crime, unable to be held back as the remaining police officers no longer had time for any form of pro-active work to deter it. Information and intelligence to the police dried up as the familiar faces of well-known and trusted PCSO's and beat officers disappeared from communities. Intelligence is what helps the police to locate those most at risk of radicalisation to terrorism or grooming by criminal gangs.

Sadly the events of the protest march were overshadowed by the coach journey home. My rota had been on a night shift the night immediately prior and had 'ghosted' the day of the march – staying awake for all of the following day. After the parade had finished, we had a couple of hours before needing to get back on our coach so all had a few beers. The drink clearly had an additional effect on all of us given how tired we already were and many of us, including myself, fell asleep on the coach back. A couple of officers however didn't, including one who was always a bit of a 'jack-the-lad'. During the coach journey at some point on the way back, this officer 'teabagged' a colleague who was asleep - essentially, putting his scrotum into the mouth of the sleeping colleague. These pair were good friends out of work and there was much made later of the incident being a sexual offence. The 'victim' of the matter didn't consider it that, and apparently actually found it quite funny when he was woken up by it, but clearly the bosses didn't. Another officer who had a previous long-standing disagreement with the offending officer, reported what they had heard of the incident to the Professional Standards Department (PSD).

After our days off we all returned to work and were in the morning briefing when officers from the PSD came in and took everyone out the room who had been on the London trip. We were taken to several different police stations and sat in isolation. One by one they took statements from us and denied us representation from our staff representatives at the Police Federation, telling us we were witnesses and so didn't require them. I wasn't sure what they actually wanted a statement about as they wouldn't tell me what they were investigating. I therefore gave a statement detailing going to London, marching, coming home and falling asleep.

It was only after I'd spent an hour with them giving a seven A4 pages statement essentially about nothing, that I came out and was allowed to speak to another colleague. She told me that she believed the PSD were investigating the 'teabagging' incident. I'd been asleep at the time this happened, so not having seen it directly I'd not mentioned it in my previous statement – statements are legally only supposed to be events that the statement-giver has directly witnessed themself.

I was then concerned that it might look like I was covering something up and so spoke to one of the PSD officers and provided them a second statement about an incident of which I had only heard third-hand and not witnessed. The 'victim' of the incident was apparently pressured extensively to make a criminal complaint of sexual assault, which he refused to do. There was also a lot of talk that any officers on the bus of Sergeant rank or higher were under investigation for failure to supervise – in spite of them all being off-duty. The way in which the PSD handled both the supposed witnesses and the victim caused significant amounts of ill-feeling towards them by all involved and remained with me for the large part of my career.

The officer responsible was ultimately fired for gross misconduct. Whether their dismissal was justified or not has been the subject of discussion for the entire length of my service amongst officers who were aware of it. On the one hand, activities like that take place on sports tours or 'initiation ceremonies' for various student groups or similar day-in, day-out across the country; and on the other, it's not the actions of a professional disciplined organisation on a work-organised event, to a colleague who was asleep at the time. It also caused some mistrust of the officer who reported it. Especially when it transpired he'd been asking colleagues questions about the incident and secretly recording them on his phone in order to support his report to the PSD.

***

My new ability to respond to incidents on blue lights also meant that often on day and afternoon shifts I was single-crewed or paired up with a colleague who wasn't a response driver. This provided me a great freedom to patrol where I wanted and police how I wanted. During my probation I'd been lucky to work fairly regularly with some very pro-active cops who enjoyed hunting for baddies and trying to prevent or detect crime that might otherwise go unnoticed - such as drugs or carrying weapons. This had developed a passion for pro-activeness within me too, and being able to police how I wanted allowed me to develop this passion. This pro-activity was ultimately to lead later in my career to my favourite role in the police. At this time though I needed to hone that skill and develop it as much as possible. It also led to some of the most interesting incidents I dealt with in my time in the police.

Certainly one of the most bizarre incidents through the length of my service involved a fairly routine traffic stop one evening in Radford. I was on patrol when I noticed a car with a particularly fogged-up windscreen – to the extent that the driver wouldn't have been able to see out and I certainly couldn't see in. It was late evening time, dark and having fogged-up windows is often a sign of a drink driver. At the very least it's an accident waiting to happen, so I turned my police car around and pulled them over. I got out and went to speak to the driver who locked his car doors, refused to open his window and declined to provide any information about himself. Checks of the vehicle against police computers showed that it was apparently uninsured and had no registered keeper, so I couldn't work out who he might have been that way.

He eventually opened his window about an inch so that we could hear one another better and I tried to explain why I had stopped him and ask for his details. He kept responding by asking me what law I was dealing with him under and what powers I had to stop him undertaking his "lawful travelling". I informed him that Section 163 of the Road Traffic Act allows police officers to stop any vehicle on a road, and Sections 164 and 165 allow them to check driving licences and insurance. His response to that was that "the Road Traffic Act is an Act, not a Law" and that he was "not travelling for a commercial purpose and therefore free to come and go as I choose without entering into any contract with the State". He also kept asking me if I was "acting under my Oath as a Constable" and to recite it to him.

These phrases immediately identified him as a 'Freeman of the Land'. This is a strange belief system that really came to prominence around this time. A small group of what would probably be termed 'conspiracy theorists' decided that in essence, if they did not consent to the law, they did not have to abide by it. Their reasoning was largely centred around the fact that the policing model in the UK is called 'policing by consent' and therefore if they didn't consent, they didn't need to be dealt with by the police. Unfortunately for their hair-brained theory the consent is by the majority of the population, not specific individuals. What criminal would otherwise consent to being arrested?! They also generally do not believe that any legislation made by the government (Acts of Parliament) are valid as they have not consented to it. To top it all off, for some reason the only law they recognise is the Magna Carta. Just for clarification at this point, once an Act is passed in Parliament and the House of Lords and given Royal Assent it becomes Law, so there is no difference between the two in practical terms.

Our conversation went round in circles for some half an hour, with him asking the same questions and me patiently explaining the way the legal system works and my powers. (Sometimes knowing a few bits of legislation, especially powers to stop vehicles, can be very helpful for police officers, particularly if you're pro-actively minded. People often demand to know why you've stopped them and refuse to give you their details. I've found that if you know the powers you have to require their information it can often achieve your aim very quickly. Sadly not in this case.)

After half an hour and having never encountered such a situation before, I was unsure what action I could take for what was essentially a minor road traffic offence. I contacted my Sergeant who came to join me and he tried to speak to the driver, again without success. He then reminded me that we can arrest anyone for any offence if the 'necessity criteria' are met – one of which being if we can't establish the person's identity. Police can also use reasonable force to exercise any of their powers if it's necessary and justifiable. Left with no other option, I went through one last appeal with the driver who *still* would not comply. I took out my extendable ASP baton, 'racked' it and smashed the passenger window. Reaching in, I unlocked the car and informed the driver he was under arrest – all for having an obstructed windscreen and on suspicion of having no insurance.

When we got to custody the driver still refused to provide any details. He had no ID on him and perhaps even more bizarrely his fingerprints were not known, showing he'd never been arrested before. Whilst booking him in I remembered the main reason why I had stopped the car in the first place and requested the driver give me a breath sample. Of course he refused to comply with this either so I arrested him for that too – failing to provide a specimen means a mandatory driving ban.

Because we could not work out who he was, he was left in the cell overnight for officers the following morning to try and reason with him after a time for him to reflect. He still refused to tell them, but they found a casino card in his property which they took the casino, who had a picture of him and his name and address on their systems. He was therefore charged with failing to provide a breath sample, driving with no insurance and the obstructed windscreen offence and bailed to court.

Clearly he wasn't going to admit these offences as he didn't recognise the laws under which he had been charged. My Sergeant and I were duly called to court a few months later and were quite surprised when the defendant actually turned up. As he was called into the actual court room for the hearing though, the fun and games continued. He walked literally to the carpet line at the door of the room and began speaking to the District Judge from there, asking "what authority do you have to hold a court here?" "Have you been appointed by the people and have the people given you authority to judge them, because I don't recognise that authority?" A District Judge is not the person to try this tactic with as they are experienced legal professionals, unlike Magistrates who are lay people with only minimal legal training. Especially this District Judge, Judge Pyle, who would commonly historically be referred to as a 'hanging judge' as he does not tolerate time-wasters and quite rightly harshly punishes those who take cases to court where the evidence against them is overwhelming.

After the driver had made these requests of the judge he was given an ultimatum to come into the court room or be dealt with more stringently. The male still refused to enter so Judge Pyle summoned my Sergeant and me into the room and said "Officers, the defendant has failed to appear in my court for trial and therefore I am issuing a warrant for his arrest. Should you find him, please return him before this court as promptly as possible". My Sergeant and I looked at each other and then at the defendant who was stood just behind us – but crucially outside of the actual court room – and I then went straight over and arrested him. I walked him round to the police custody suite which was right next door to the court building and my Sergeant joined me a few minutes later with the signed warrant from the judge. I got some very funny looks from the custody Sergeant when I explained I had arrested the male for failing to appear at court; "place of arrest?", "Nottingham Magistrates' Court"! He was booked in and then sent straight through to the court's processing area whilst my Sergeant and I went back upstairs to wait in the court room.

The defendant was brought up into the dock by the security staff where the judge asked him to confirm his name and address which he still refused to do. Judge Pyle again gave him an ultimatum that if he did not provide the required details, he would be held in contempt of court. The male still refused, so the judge quite casually sentenced him to two months imprisonment! Just as the security officers were taking him downstairs back to the court cells to await transport to prison, a meek voice called up "OK, OK, I'll give you my details." The judge rescinded the previous sentence and then said:

"Whilst I was waiting for these officers to return you to the court I have read through their statements and the case file and cannot see that there is anything you could say in your defence that would alter the facts of this case. I therefore find you guilty of the offences charged, I cannot take any guilty plea into account and as you have not provided a statement of your means I cannot balance your income against any punishment."

He then handed down the stiffest sentence I have ever witnessed for minor road traffic matters, including a multiple year ban from driving alongside a hefty fine nearing £1000 and community service! The driver gets full marks for conviction to his principles, but no marks for absurdity in the face of clear overwhelming facts against you. To top it all off, I'd been with a special constable at the time of the stop who I was tutoring. Not only was this one of the first incidents that he encountered in his policing career, but it was also the one and only time he was required to attend court. I'm very disappointed that he didn't get to see that it wasn't always like this occasion!

The bizarreness of that day wasn't over yet either. My Sergeant and I were leaving court, him in his own car and me in a police car, when he called to me and asked "did you see that?". I didn't know what he meant so he explained he had seen a male coming out of a side door from the custody suite and running out the vehicle gates of the compound when a car came in. I waited whilst he went back into the custody suite and sure enough a detainee was missing! A full-scale search rapidly swung into action. Calls from members of the public about a male stealing clothes from a line and heading into the nearby Park Estate suggested which way the male had gone. Every unit from the city and beyond travelled to the area and the whole estate was essentially closed off. I was just in a white shirt and tie having attended court, with none of my equipment belt, just a radio. After about an hour of searching with the helicopter and dogs the male was located hiding in a bush in a garden. It transpired that he had been left waiting in the corridor on his own for a minute by an officer and had found a side door through a rarely used office. This led to a staff corridor where he found a fire exit that led into the staff car park and that's how he had got out. All his efforts ultimately got him was an extra charge of escaping lawful custody.

It's never made sense to me why people 'go on the run' or try and avoid the police in cases where their identity is known. It's almost a certainty that the police will catch up with you at some point and surely it's better to just get whatever the issue is over and done with? Often people spend longer 'on the run' trying to avoid police than the outcome of any court case would affect them for, and it must be a life of constantly looking over your shoulder. They must be aware that anyone they have a fall-out with could report them to the police at any moment, and always have to be conscious not to register any vehicles or addresses in their real name. Perhaps my favourite part is that it generally prevents them from ever leaving the country. If a wanted person tries to get on a plane or a boat their name flags up and they get arrested at the border. The best example of this was towards the end of my career when I was a Sergeant. I was informed that a male who had been wanted for some six months had checked-in to a long-haul flight leaving Heathrow. It was obvious that he was well aware he was wanted and had chosen to actively avoid police for that entire time. Unfortunately for him his efforts to avoid us led to me requesting the Heathrow Airport police arrest him. His no doubt quite expensive plane ticket was completely wasted after he was taken out the queue for boarding at the gate and brought back to Nottingham for questioning!

***

Sometimes bizarre situations arise out of people's mistakes. We all make them. One of the biggest errors that I witnessed followed a call to a high-end car garage for reports that the alarm had gone off. My colleague and I arrived and checked round the outside, not seeing any signs of damage or forced entry. As we looked round we got near to the entrance door and all of a sudden it just opened for us! We had obviously stepped on the pressure plate outside and triggered the door's opening mechanism. Only, it was late at night and the garage was closed. Concerned that someone may have somehow forced entry we went into the showroom and looked round where we were joined by a security guard who had arrived with the keys.

He took us round the whole garage which not only had the new cars on display in the showroom but also numerous other prestige cars in a repair bay on the premises as well. It was a car fan's dream and of course we had to have a good look in all the cars to ensure that none had been entered or disturbed in any way... A heart-stopping moment came when my colleague who was not a car fan, was walking between two closely parked very expensive cars and a 'clunk' noise signalled the sound of his handcuffs on his kit belt knocking into one of the side panels! The security man and I instantly looked over and the guard highlighted how a scratch on the panel could cost up to £10,000 to put right on that particular car! Nicholas Cage and Vin Diesel would have had a much easier time of *Gone in 60 Seconds* if the forgetful staff member who had forgotten to lock the garage's doors had been at work the day they did their giant 'boost'.

***

Road traffic matters are often viewed by police officers as being fairly trivial and cops are often firmly in two camps of those who 'do traffic' and those who don't. I was most assuredly in the first camp, absolutely passionate about how dealing with seemingly minor offences such as using a mobile phone or speeding can save lives. This was abjectly demonstrated in one incident where the control room had received a series of calls about a possible drunk driver heading into Nottingham from the M1. The driver had collided with pavements, other cars and street furniture and was heading to our patch. Clearly the car needed stopping and a call to us a short time later confirmed it had stopped of its own accord on the city's ring road, blocking a lane. Several colleagues and I arrived to ensure the safety of the area as well as tried to speak to the driver. He was slumped over the steering wheel but was swaying and as we tried to talk to him he initially gave us the middle finger and then turned the volume up on the stereo, closing and locking the doors when we tried to open them. Clearly we needed to get this male out and stop him driving any further and our suspicion at this time was that he was under the influence of drink or drugs.

Breaking a car window and getting the keys is a lot harder than it sounds. It's one of the most dangerous activities police officers can undertake. It is particularly on the minds of Nottinghamshire officers after the tragic death in 2003 of dog handler PC Ged Walker, who was killed after being dragged along by a car that he had reached inside to try and take the keys from. With this in mind we used our police cars to create a box around the suspect vehicle, blocking it bumper to bumper at front, rear and alongside the driver's door so it couldn't drive off. I offered to be the one to go in, which was potentially dangerous not only for the driver being able to attempt to ram his way out if he chose, but he was also of a very muscular build and had shown active hostility to us. I put the passenger window through with my ASP and unlocked the door from inside, before climbing in over the broken glass, CS canister in hand. The driver offered no resistance and I managed to take the keys out of the ignition, before climbing back out. We then moved the police cars to get access to the driver's side and between several of us and using body pivot point techniques, managed to get the resisting male out the car.

Whilst we were doing this, another colleague was searching the car for any clues as to the cause of the man's condition. In the boot they found an insulin injection kit, and after letting us know about this, our concerns around him changed from criminal to medical. Thankfully another officer with us had thought to request an ambulance whilst we were with him due to his apparent level of intoxication, and so we sat him in the rear of that and he was checked over. The paramedics confirmed that he had exceptionally low blood sugar levels.

He was given some insulin and was interviewed at a later date for careless driving and ultimately found guilty at court based on the fact that he would have been fully aware his blood sugars were dipping, and had actively chosen not to stop and eat a chocolate bar or use his insulin injection that was in the car. The DVLA revoked his licence as well on medical grounds following a police referral.

The male made a complaint to the police and sued the force for the loss of his licence. Whilst this was going through, he continued to drive, contrary to his licence revocation and a year or so later crashed in very similar circumstances. Tragically in this instance, his car left the road at speed and he died. This incident proved a big learning experience for my colleagues and me in that the presentation of diabetic episodes is remarkably similar to drunkenness. I was always sure to relate this anecdote to colleagues at similar incidents in future, to increase their awareness and pause for consideration. We learnt about it in training, but until you experience it first hand, it's easy to overlook.

Urgent medical episodes are a not-uncommon part of the job as a police officer, either where people are injured as a result of criminal action, assisting the ambulance service at potentially volatile situations, or mental health-related crises. Less common is the incident that I was faced with one summer's Sunday. Whilst on routine patrol I was flagged down outside St Barnabus' Cathedral on Derby Road by a priest in his full vestments. I pulled up next to him and wound the window down.

"Excuse me, we've called an ambulance, but can you help? We finished service about 20 minutes ago and I've just finished seeing everyone off, but one of the parishioners is sat in his car there, slumped over the wheel and we can't get a response from him".

This instantly set some alarm bells ringing so I got out the police car and went to look at the chap in question. I could see that the car occupant's lips were a definite shade of bluey/grey, and knocking on his window and shouting got no response. Thankfully his doors weren't locked so I opened them and, checking for breathing or a pulse as per my first aid training, I found neither. I dragged the male out of the car with some difficulty, put him onto the floor and requested for more officers and an ambulance to join me ASAP. I threw the priest my car keys and asked him to get the first aid kit out the boot. For the first time ever I then began doing chest compressions, muscle memory taking over thanks to the regular first aid training we received. The priest returned and got me out a face shield so I continued to do CPR and giving breaths.

Anyone who has ever had the extreme misfortune to have been in a position of needing to give another person CPR will know how distressing it can be. The ribs crack under the pressure of the first few compressions and it also gets tiring very quickly – especially in restrictive police body armour. Unfortunately for me my radio earpiece fell out with the violent movement, so I couldn't hear the dispatcher asking for more information from me. Luckily a colleague apparently realised what was likely going on and several units travelled to me, including an armed response vehicle who are equipped with defibrillators. They arrived and connected the device, which would not provide shocks as it did not register the required pulses from the heart, so I continued to give CPR.

The ambulance still hadn't arrived and it later turned out after their eventual arrival that there were two St Barnabus' churches in Nottingham, both on Derby Road, but the other near Priory Island. The ambulances had initially been dispatched to the other one and it was several minutes before the error had been realised. Even after they arrived they asked me to continue CPR whilst they connected all their equipment, meaning by the time they took over, I had been doing compressions and breaths for some 20 – 25 minutes. I was exhausted. It was only about another minute or two later that the ambulance crew sadly pronounced the male deceased.

The priest was able to give the devoutly religious deceased man the Last Rites. Speaking to the priest it was evident that the man was a well-respected and popular member of the congregation as well as a reasonably well-known musician who played music for the church and in the community. It was then my sad duty to inform his next of kin of his passing. At least I was able to tell them that I had done everything that I possibly could to try and save his life. I think it was a comfort to them that he had just been to church which he enjoyed, and that the priest was on hand and able to bless him at the moment of his passing, which is what he would have wanted. There is now a memorial plaque to this man in one of the pubs in the city where I occasionally drink. I see the memorial there as a reminder of that day, which I look back on with sadness but also a sense that I'd done everything I possibly could for him.

As a post-script to this incident, the very next day I was on my way to a routine enquiry when I saw a car stopped in a lay-by at the side of the road and the driver was slumped over the wheel! Not believing that my luck could be that bad, I stopped next to him and went to bang on the window. Thankfully on this occasion the male sat up and looked wide-eyed at me, not able to process in his immediate post-sleep state why there was a police officer stood at his window. I explained the situation from yesterday and he laughed, telling me he was just grabbing 40 winks after a long drive and that he was fine, but thanked me for my concern!

This is another incident that stayed with me ever since and is another location I can't go past without remembering what happened there each and every time. It's no wonder that exposed to such traumatic occurrences on a regular basis, the rate of mental health crises among police officers is so high. Forces pay lip-service to mental health concerns in their workforce, but the anecdotal experiences of so many colleagues who have suffered at the hands of the 'black dog' suggests the support available is not meaningful or long-lasting. Sadly the Austerity measures from the government must bear the responsibility of this epidemic, by forcing police officers to "do more with less" as Theresa May so famously said when she was Home Secretary driving the savage cuts. Police officers are humans, with real emotions and limits of how much they can realistically individually achieve.

Dealing with death is never a pleasant experience as there are always other people – friends and relatives – who lose the person close to them. It can also be unpleasant for other reasons. The human body decays reasonably rapidly, is not pleasant to deal with after even a few days and gets rapidly worse from there. Later in my career when I was a Sergeant I was required to attend all unexpected deaths to ensure as far as possible that there were no suspicious circumstances. I saw a lot of bodies, several in an advanced state of decay. It's also a sad personal experience for attending officers, or at least that's what I found. The officer often only meets the person after they've died, but can actually get to know them quite well to a degree as a result of having to go through their property to find next of kin details and secure any valuables: sadly there are a minority of people out there who see undertakers arriving at a house and view the newly empty property as an easy burglary opportunity. Some of the most tragic deaths the police attend are those where people have chosen to end their own life, often as a result of mental health related issues.

On one occasion I was in the Radford area when I saw British Transport Police officers blue-lighting around to various railway access points. After seeing them a couple of times, I went to ask what they were looking for and if I could help. They told me they'd had reports of a man been hit by a train nearby and they were looking for the scene. We walked onto the railway lines where we were (after confirmation that the trains had been stopped!) and ran up the tracks for about a mile until we found the train.

When we got to the train it was only a single-carriage local service, but the damage it had done to the person it had hit was horrific. Body parts were spread out over several hundred yards from the point of impact near to a bridge. Several other BTP officers including an Inspector arrived after we had identified the nearest access point. He assessed the scene and spoke to the driver. He told us that the man had stepped out from behind the bridge right at the last minute before the train passed it, so there was nothing the driver could have done to avoid the collision.

We located an ID card and I was able to check our local databases which showed that the dead man had suffered from severe depression for many years. The Inspector concluded that the male had committed suicide. A body recovery kit was brought to us which the BTP apparently routinely carry around with them, so frequently do they deal with situations like this. The other officers and I got to work collecting all the body parts we could locate, including eyes and brain matter, placing it all into the bag which the BTP officers took to the mortuary. It was a really clinical display of efficiency from the officers who deal with such unfortunate circumstances on a regular basis, whilst being done with utmost respect for the dead person. The officers must become hardened to such horror to some degree, but this can't be good for their own mental wellbeing. It's also a sad indication of the point that some people must reach in their lives where they could even contemplate such an action, let alone actually carry it out. It can't even be that uncommon, as train drivers have a policy in their contracts that states if they have three people commit suicide by their trains, the drivers are eligible for medical retirement. It must be an awful experience for them as well, watching another human being stepping out in front of them and having a couple of seconds where they know that there is nothing that can do to stop the impact and inevitable consequences.

Developing my Skills

***

I've already alluded to how my passion lay in pro-active policing, using any opportunity available to stop vehicles and deal with whatever I encountered, be it minor road traffic offences or criminal matters. This initial foray into exploring pro-active work was to lead me to the biggest job of my early career that I'd discovered for myself. It's a job of which I remain very proud and it inspired in me a passion for this kind of work leading me to my future career path. It was also indirectly to lead, several years later, to violence and tragedy.

I was out on a patrol with a colleague on a weekend evening where the afternoon shift started and finished later so as to provide extra cover for the busy periods of the city's 'Night Time Economy'. As I didn't directly cover the city centre at this time, we were rarely requested to attend incidents there as the city response and dedicated NTE teams would be able to manage most of it. This allowed us time to undertake pro-active work because the night shift would cover the normal demand.

We became suspicious of a car that had three young males in. Initially we spotted it driving slowly down a predominantly student street, but on seeing us it sped up and drove out the area. Checks with the control room suggested that the keeper of the vehicle was linked to drugs so we stopped it, and sure enough as we spoke to the occupants a smell of cannabis was apparent from inside. Based on their demeanour with us, the intelligence and the smell of cannabis, we searched the car and the occupants. Each one of the three had around £400 in cash and there were also a couple of mobile phones that kept ringing. When more colleagues arrived we undertook a more thorough search of the car and found half a dozen wraps of what looked like class A drugs hidden in a void.

We arrested the occupants for being concerned in the supply of class A, seized the drugs, cash and phones, took them to custody and had searches of their addresses authorised. By this time we were already late off, but you don't mind when it's a good job. There were three addresses to do, so they were divided up between the shift, and I went to one with a couple of colleagues. In the address was a car key and a V5 vehicle logbook. A check of surrounding streets located the car detailed on the logbook parked unattended nearby. A further search authority was granted for the car and in the boot we found a bag-for-life full of what appeared to be a significant quantity of more class A drugs and boxes of business cards. These business cards are used by drug dealers to give to their customers with normally just their phone number on, so the users know who to call but that doesn't explicitly say 'drugs' on it so they can't directly be prosecuted for offering drugs for sale.

The drugs recovered turned out to be 400g of MDMA (ecstasy) worth about £12,000 at that time. Evidence from their phones showed that the trio had been dealing drugs across the city for some considerable time. I attended the sentencing hearing at court on my day off, to witness them each get sentenced to two year's imprisonment, despite having no previous convictions which was quite a good outcome. Sadly the economics of drug dealing meant that they now owed someone else this £12,000 which was to later lead to serious consequences.

One of these three – the one who was storing the drugs – said at court that he had previously bought cannabis off the other two and then had no money to buy more. In order to get more cannabis without having the cash he had agreed to store drugs for them in lieu of payment and then began using the class A drugs that they supplied as well. This showed to me the fact that cannabis is a frequently a gateway drug, especially for the young and vulnerable, into both taking and selling harder more dangerous narcotics. I have also seen first-hand the effects that cannabis can have on the mental health of some people who consume it, especially in significant quantities.

One occasion that was to profoundly demonstrate that was when I was dispatched to a casino in town. Police had received reports that a male had stolen a walkie-talkie off one of the door staff and was running off with it, with the security guards in pursuit. When I got there the thief had already been detained by the security and as soon as I spoke to him it was immediately apparent that he was in some kind of mental health crisis. He was saying things along the lines of:

"Thank God you're here. I need to be arrested. The seven most powerful people in the world are after me and nowhere is safe. I borrowed 100 million pounds off them and now they want it back and I don't have it. They've got people everywhere and I need to be safe. Please arrest me and take me somewhere safe."

I arrested the male on suspicion of theft and have never seen anyone so happy to be taken into custody. He was convinced that he was safe in the police cells and that the "seven most powerful people in the world" could not get to him and kill him in there. It might sound harsh to arrest someone seemingly having a mental health crisis, but in custody someone's mental health can be checked by professionals and the case discontinued if they really are unwell. Sometimes people feign mental illness in an attempt to avoid being arrested.

He turned out to be only seventeen which meant I had to visit his parents and inform them of his arrest. They told me that their son had been smoking more and more cannabis recently and they had seen a marked decrease in his mental state, with him becoming increasingly paranoid and apparently schizophrenic. After his mental health assessment in custody he was detained at a mental health facility for help and treatment and no charges were pressed against him due to his health crisis.

Advocates of legalising cannabis often say to me that it is harmless and even beneficial. Maybe to most people it probably is fairly harmless if smoked in small quantities, and certainly no worse than alcohol. Users just cannot know though if they have genes that mean it will cause them to develop severe neurological issues, and to me that's not worth the risk – either to them, the health service or the general public. It is also often used as a 'gateway drug' to more serious ones.

***

In early 2013 I was recovering from an illness that had seen me off work for several months. A dodgy takeaway had given me food poisoning, which developed into Campylobacter, which in turn gave me gastroenteritis. I then found out I was blessed with some rare genes which meant that the antibodies created to fight the inflammation in my digestive system don't die off as they should once they completed their task. Instead, they attack other areas of inflammation in the body, which through the body's normal use and movement is the joints. As a result of this auto-immune disease I was diagnosed with Reactive Arthritis and for some three months or more it was all I could do on a daily basis to crawl from my bed to the sofa. Luckily this is an ailment with a fixed lifespan of around a year, so after six months I was back to work on restricted duties and some intensive physiotherapy and exercise I was back to full work after about eleven months.

I'd always felt strongly about a couple of the founding principles of the police as purportedly laid down by Sir Robert Peel who said that "the primary duty of the police is to prevent crime and disorder"; and that "the test of police efficiency is the absence of crime and disorder, not the visible evidence of the police dealing with them". With these ideals in mind, during night shifts on my recuperative duties, when there was little need for admin work, I would take an unmarked car out and patrol crime hotspots, checking any vehicles I saw or requesting uniformed officers come and stop suspicious individuals.

One night I was driving around Wollaton, which was experiencing a spate of burglaries at that time. A car with three young men in it caught my eye as I saw it turn into one of the smaller housing estates. I knew that the road they'd turned onto looped round the small estate and had only the one entrance / exit point. I drove in and turned the other way, knowing that if the vehicle passed me it had no purpose in being there – it meant it would have driven more than half the estate when it would have been quicker to go the opposite direction. Sure enough I got passed by the car going the other way, which massively raised my suspicions. I let it go past and then turned around, caught up behind it and checked the registration number, which showed as being registered and insured to only a woman. I requested a marked unit come and stop the car, but my colleagues were some distance away meaning I had to follow it for a while.

Unlike in Hollywood films, if you follow a car for more than a few streets at night, it's very obvious to the person being followed that that's what you're doing, especially if they turn off a main road and you continue behind them. They were quickly aware they were being tailed despite my best efforts and started to speed up significantly. I updated over the radio and several other units including traffic officers started converging on my location. I kept up with the vehicle as long as I could but it was travelling very fast by this point and making regular turns so I soon lost it. I was also very aware that I did not have blue lights or sirens in my unmarked car to warn other motorists or pedestrians who might be out.

The helicopter and dog units were also heading my way and after a short search of the area the car was found parked abandoned with the doors open near to Wollaton Park. The dog unit went to the location along with the helicopter and the eyes-in-the-sky soon identified three heat sources running across the park. The police dog was sent after them and bit two, with the third detained by officers. I went to the car and searched it, finding gloves, balaclavas and screwdrivers – all the equipment budding burglars would need. All three were arrested for going equipped to steal and the driver for having no insurance and disqualified driving. I believe at least two of them had previous convictions for burglary, they weren't from the area and couldn't account for why they were in this neighbourhood.

Unfortunately I don't think any were charged except the driver for some traffic offences, due to a lack of evidence – it's not necessarily proof of intention to steal having balaclavas, gloves and some screwdrivers in the car. They might have simply been mechanics working in the cold or similar. What I do know though is that the spate of burglaries in the area stopped after that night, which told me all I needed to know about the impact this incident had had. At least a couple of those from the car had received some 'summary justice' from the police dog as some form of punishment, and the car was taken off the road as a result of not being insured.

My desire to be pro-active and my hope to be more independent, make a bigger impact and a meaningful difference to the community as an individual led me to take my next career move. A vacancy was advertised for 'beat managers' to join the team at Canning Circus police station, covering the area that I was familiar with and loved working from my time on response. I jumped at the opportunity.

Neighbourhood Policing

"It's not all slippers, hugging babies and Dundee cakes"

After five years on response I felt it was time for a change and successfully applied for a position as a beat manager on the Safer Neighbourhoods Team, based out of Canning Circus Police Station. The beat manager role enabled me to continue policing the area that I loved, but gave me significant scope to make more of an impact as an individual police officer through being able to manage my own workload and target areas that I wanted linked to priorities identified by residents. I would have more time to problem solve issues in my area, as well as take ownership of ongoing threats and risks on my beat. I remained as a beat manager for only two years, but during that time I had probably the greatest single achievement of my career in terms of community impact, and also some of my biggest arrests. Previous incidents would also come back to rear their heads in new ways as well.

***

I certainly staked my colours to the mast within the first few weeks of being in the role. I very quickly identified several properties where drugs were being grown and / or dealt from and obtained warrants for them all, executing these at a rate of probably one a week for several months. I became very familiar with the search teams and police drugs experts as a result of this work, as well as the intelligence department who would often contact me asking me to firm up intelligence that they had received or to try and help bolster intelligence gaps.

I also began to make my name amongst the local baddies, quickly identifying a street where the local postcode-based gang would hang out. Patrolling this area gave me a wealth of intelligence by getting car registration numbers and being able to link them to the people using them as I got to know more and more of the gang members. My regular presence at the location became a real annoyance to them, and there was more than one occasion where someone from the gang made indirect threats to my safety or even my life if I kept going round there and 'harassing' them.

The idea of police harassment is quite funny to me, because if you're a law-abiding member of the public, you're very unlikely to encounter a police officer in your life unless you're a victim of crime. If you feel harassed by the police, it represents a significant focus of scant resources in your direction, so you must be doing something to warrant that level of police attention! The name of 'PC Tom Andrews' became almost a bogey-man amongst certain elements of the community I worked in, with myself and another colleague known as 'Raddy Steve' being specifically brought up in community meetings as seemingly being everywhere all the time. Before the force insisted on putting our names on our epaulettes, the local baddies would constantly repeat my name to me as another way to attempt to intimidate me; as if by knowing my name they felt they somehow had power over me. To a degree this can be true, as in today's society everyone is traceable online, but simple measures such as using alias names on social media can thwart all but the most determined effort to find you.

Over the course of a year or so I would regularly park my police car on the street they hung out on and use the new internet-enabled laptop (the only one at the station!) to complete my admin work. I would get regular intelligence of criminal associations from these visits by seeing who was hanging out with who. When none of the gang were there, some of the more law-abiding residents would come and thank me for being there regularly and give me more information about what was happening. Through the year I steadily built a picture of who the regular faces there were. I would also collate the regular incidents of anti-social behaviour called in from the residents which mostly related to this same group. The calls to police included reports of street drinking late into the night with music being played; car related nuisance; drug use; and around November, fireworks being let off towards cars and houses.

After gathering this evidence, I used brand new powers under the Anti-Social Behaviour, Crime and Policing Act, only brought in a few months prior, to issue Community Protection Notices (CPN) to half a dozen of the key individuals. This gave them legal notice not to loiter on the street; not to consume alcohol in the area; and not to cause nuisance to any residents of the street. This solved the problem overnight and I never saw the group on that street again. I made sure to let the residents know by delivering letters to all the houses on the street explaining what I had done and encouraging them to report any anti-social behaviour so the police could attend and deal with any breaches of the CPN's. We didn't get any calls about further ASB and I also received feedback at subsequent community meetings that the quality of the residents' lives had been significantly improved. This is exactly what I had become a beat manager to do – both fight potential crime by accumulating intelligence around identified gang-related individuals and improve the lives of the community on my beat area. Having now become a lecturer in policing at a university, teaching new student officers, I use this situation as a case-study for how to tackle ongoing anti-social behaviour in a community.

***

That example of problem solving was not even my proudest achievement during my time as a beat manager. That came from a much bigger operation that took place on one day, rather than over a period of time. 2015 was a time when New Psychoactive Substances (NPS) were grabbing national headlines but were more commonly referred to by their colloquial name – 'legal highs'. These were artificially manufactured drugs intended to be synthetic versions of all the well-known narcotics. Chemically they were subtly different however, in order to circumvent the law which only related to the specific chemical compounds of cannabis, MDMA, cocaine etc. The issue with these new items was that there was no clear description or knowledge of the effects of each subtly different type of drug. They could be sold openly over the counter in shops as they were "not illegal" and this did result in instances nationally of naïve young people trying them and dying from the effects, or becoming addicted to them. It was also driving a national epidemic of so-called Spice- or Mamba-zombies – people who took these substances and went into an almost catatonic state for an hour or so as a result of the unknown, unchecked quality of the contents and quantity of the active ingredient in them.

Because the substances at this time were legal there was a real struggle for police or other agencies nationally to be able to combat the problem. On my neighbourhood area I'd identified that there were two 'head-shops' (stores that sell drug paraphernalia such as bongs, cannabis grinders etc) who were openly selling these legal highs over the counter for £10 each, or 3 for £25. The zombies and overdoses were becoming more of an issue in the area, which was noticeable on reviews of the incidents called into police on a daily basis. I spoke to my Inspector and sought permission to research a way to tackle the problem, which I was granted.

It was obvious that the police alone could not resolve the issue, so I did extensive internet trawls and found that previously in Nottingham the Council's Trading Standards department had seized a quantity of NPS from sale as being unsafe goods. I contacted them and quickly established a good working relationship with one of the team members there. We held several planning sessions where we decided that Trading Standards could indeed seize the items as being 'unsafe goods' and then seek a court order for their destruction. The rationale behind this was that the packets were sold with no contents listed, no stated intended purpose (other than saying on them they were "not fit for human consumption"!) and no details of who to contact in the event of any incident with them or manufacturer details. Trading Standards powers were quite extensive with regards to unsafe goods being offered for sale. They could enter any retail premises and seize goods they suspected to be unsafe, without a warrant. This didn't permit the police to be involved or result in any criminal proceedings. Crucially it also didn't necessarily prevent the problem recurring if the shopkeepers just bought more stock and continued to sell them until they were raided again.

In order to facilitate police involvement, I came across Section 9A of the Misuse of Drugs Act. This little-known bit of legislation makes it an offence to supply paraphernalia intended to be used for the consumption of drugs. That was clearly what these shops were doing and had been for quite some time. I managed to obtain warrants for both the shops and the owners' home addresses based on this section of the legislation and a recent successful prosecution using it in another force area.

Given that we would be searching four premises at the same time I began planning a large-scale policing operation. I requested specialist search teams to help execute the warrants of the owners' home addresses, and additional teams in conjunction with Trading Standards to attend the shops. In what was also believed to be a national first of its kind, I took along accredited Drugs Experts to the shops. These are experienced police officers who receive extensive training in the street use of drugs, such as values and how they are made and consumed, in addition to their wealth of knowledge of dealing with and investigating drugs offences. They came along to the shops and rather than seizing all the items in each one, filmed a documentary style video at each location highlighting all the items and what their common usage would be when connected to drugs misuse. These videos could then be played at court as evidence without needing to show each individual item. The Trading Standards officers came with us and seized all the 'legal highs' from the shops – which when we got back to the police station and counted it all amounted to tens of thousands of pounds' worth.

Recognising the community impact of this 'raid' and the positive PR resulting from the visible actions of the police and Trading Standards tackling the issue, I had also pre-warned the force communications team. They in turn had arranged for the local newspaper attend with us as well. The following day's *Nottingham Evening Post* front page article was about the "Police Blitz on Legal Highs" and had a total of four pages-worth devoted to the operation.

Both shopkeepers were arrested on suspicion of supplying drugs paraphernalia. In their interviews though they came out with the stock answers that allow these 'head-shops' to remain open – that what are clearly bongs are ornamental glass vases; the cannabis grinders are herb grinders; the cannabis seeds are not illegal to sell etc and that what their customers choose to do with the items after they buy them is beyond the shop's control. This is a significant loophole in the law as a result of which they were ultimately not charged with that offence. I was able to charge one shopkeeper with selling knuckle-dusters which is illegal, and the other shopkeeper kept a can of pepper spray behind his counter so was charged with possessing that. Trading Standards did successfully apply to the court for the forfeiture and destruction of the 'legal highs' and the small fortune's worth of harmful drugs was sent to the incinerator. This was the key win that we were looking for, with any prosecution of the shop keepers only being a secondary consideration which wouldn't have necessarily achieved anything significant anyway.

The secondary focus of the operation was to combat any potential recurrence of the issue. In an alternative use of the new Community Protection Notices, I required the owners to stop selling items that could be consumed by people to cause psychoactive effects and based this instruction on the evidence of all the reports of mamba-zombies from the area over the preceding months. The shops never did again sell NPS and in testament to how profitable and dependent on sales of those items the shops were, one of the shops closed down only a few months later. Till receipts seized from the shop had shown that they were taking ten thousand pounds or more a month from the sales of these harmful substances in 'legalised drug dealing'. Like all drug dealers, the sellers clearly didn't care about the effects of their products on their customers.

In the following months I received calls from several officers around the country who had come across the newspaper article during their own research to tackle the problem on their areas. I was only too happy to share my experiences as this operation, which is probably the thing of which I am most proud in my policing career overall. I feel that the impact it had at the time on improving the health and wellbeing of the community was head and shoulders above anything else an individual PC is normally able to achieve. The government thankfully made these awful substances illegal only two years later.

Anyone who argues in favour of the legalisation of drugs would do well to look at the NPS phenomenon as a case study. Because the items were legal, naïve people bought them quite legitimately over the counter, not knowing at all what was in them. Even Viagra was more tightly controlled than these substances at the time. There is plenty of documented evidence from this period prior to the Psychoactive Substances Act 2016 detailing how Spice and Mamba ruined the lives of previously healthy people. These users had bought them thinking that because they were legal they were relatively harmless like 'poppers' or similar. Instead the users became the equivalent of Class A drug addicts, constantly seeking their next fix and ruining every part of their lives. To this day the Mamba and Spice family of synthetic cannabinoids are still only Class B drugs. This compares them in harm to cannabis and ketamine. The evidence of their impact on the user and society at large is clearly more significant than those two drugs, but there appears no appetite to increase their classification. Persons caught dealing mamba will often only face a custodial sentence on their second or third conviction and the mark up on the product is massive, encouraging this as an attractive illegal career path.

***

Alongside the more serious aspects I had many humorous moments during my time as a beat manager, as in any other role that I undertook in the police. It's often said that police officers need humour to get by, to help combat the suffering and trauma that they encounter. Sometimes this can take the form of black humour which is reserved exclusively for within the walls of the station or at the very least out of earshot of any members of the public. It's not that police officers are callous or heartless, but simple psychology shows that the brain needs to make light of extreme suffering to be able to better cope with and overcome it. This black humour is obviously very situational and relevant only at a specific time. Other comedic value occurred as a result of incidents that we were called to that can be serious at the time and funny in hindsight, or just out-and-out surreal at the time of attending.

One of the most surreal incidents that I ever attended came as a result of multiple reports to the police about a lady on a mobility scooter driving it on the city's ring road. Mobility scooters can only reach speeds little faster than walking, so to be driving it round the city's two-lane, 40mph limit, busy ring road was an accident waiting to happen. I was on my own and travelled on blue lights to get there, as did a couple of other colleagues. I was the nearest and so got there first, pulling behind the scooter with my lights and sirens on, as I typically would when signalling for a car to pull over. The lady driving it could not have cared less though and continued with her journey. I used the loudhailer function on the police car to tell her to pull off the road and stop, but again she just completely blanked me. I also tried pulling alongside, still with my blue lights on and shouted at her to stop through the passenger window. To my amazement I got a very expletive-laden response and the lady continued on her way.

My colleague and good friend Lee arrived at this point and after a brief conversation via radio we decided that we'd have to physically block her path to prevent her putting herself and other motorists at great risk. Stopping the traffic behind us, one of us then went in front of her and slowed to a stop whilst the other went alongside so she couldn't go round the one in front. Anyone who has seen any of the dramatic police TV shows should recognise the description of this manoeuvre as a box or 'TPAC'. These are normally only carried out to prevent or end high-speed pursuits and conducted by specially trained officers. In this instance though, due to the very low speeds and the significant risk to the female involved, we'd considered it quite acceptable to do ourselves. We simply parked one car in front of her and the other alongside. Mobility scooters don't have a reverse gear to the best of my knowledge.

This expertly crafted plan achieved the desired result and we could finally speak to the lady – who was *still* trying to get her scooter up on to the pavement to get away from us! It took us physically taking the key out of it before we could make sure she didn't drive off or run our feet over! It transpired she had not only some form of personality disorder, but also needed carers due to her mobility issues. For reasons only known to her and no doubt as a result of her mental health condition, she'd taken a dislike to the carer who'd come that day and decided she had to get away from the house. She was utterly determined not to go back – hence the daring four-wheeled escapade and stubborn refusal to stop for even the police. My utterly charming colleague, who was always popular with the older ladies, managed to coax her back to the address and suitable referrals were duly made to social care. Lee and I still talk about this incident to this day as one of our funniest experiences at work. There was another hilarious incident that we experienced together when we were both attached to the Knife Crime Team, but you'll have to wait for the next chapter to read about that.

This wasn't even the only bizarre mobility scooter-related incident of my career. On another occasion I successfully prosecuted someone for taking a mobility scooter without the owner's consent (TWOC) and driving it drunk! I'd been on patrol on my beat area when I saw a chap on a mobility scooter driving it down the pavement at quite a speed whilst swigging from a can of beer. He was swerving across the pavement and when I stopped and spoke to him he was clearly very drunk. He told me that he had gone to his disabled friend's house and when his friend hadn't answered the door he decided it was too far to walk back to his own house, so had taken his mobility scooter that was parked in the front garden to ride back on. He blew a fairly high reading on the roadside breathalyser, and I had to speak to the Sergeant on the roads policing team to see if a mobility scooter even legally qualified as a motor vehicle because no-one else that I spoke to had ever arrested someone for drink-driving on one! It was an offence and the guy pleaded guilty at court, getting disqualified from driving as a result; the irony here being that he didn't have a licence anyway and you don't need one to drive a mobility scooter. Police are facing similar issues today with the explosion of e-scooter use, which are also motor vehicles and require a licence, insurance and registration number to be legal. There have been several instances of riders on those being prosecuted for drink driving (riding?) and it's something to definitely for users be aware of.

***

Being on the neighbourhood team allowed a bit more time to combat local issues that cropped up from time to time, and for a month I was temporarily part of a team put together to pro-actively combat a spike in car crime, burglaries and robberies across a couple of areas. We worked in a mix of plain clothes with a uniform car as back-up and patrolled the main hotspot areas, stopping suspicious people and cars, all the while building an intelligence picture up to try and identify any possible suspects. There were six of us on the team, but at the time one of the other officers and I had a special constable each who regularly worked with us as well. As I've said before, specials are a really underrated additional police resource who give up their time for free, putting themselves in exactly the same risky situations as paid officers and doing the same job. The special I had with me at this point was really hard working and somehow balanced being an elite international gymnast and full-time university student with putting in copious hours as a special too. Jess has since gone on to become an excellent full-time officer in another force.

On this particular day the team had just paraded on duty when there was a report came in about a woman who'd had her phone stolen, then rang it and someone had answered. She'd pleaded with the person to get her phone back due to the sentimental data on it and the person who answered her call had said she could come and get it if she bought it off him for what he could otherwise sell it for. She'd agreed to this but then contacted the police to ask if there was anything we could do. We told her to come to the station which wasn't far from where the person wanted to meet her, where she explained to us that she'd arranged to go with her boyfriend to get the phone back. Jess and I were both in plain clothes so with the rest of the team we formulated a plan that she and I would pose as the victim and her boyfriend and go and meet the person trying to sell the phone. At the point the phone was offered to us we would identify ourselves as police officers and arrest the male, with the uniformed officers waiting a couple of streets away ready to head round to us to help arrest and detain him.

The plan went off perfectly. Jess and I made contact with the suspect, who we saw come out his house and meet us, showed us 'our' phone and asked for the cash. At this point I pulled out my warrant card and my handcuffs and told him he was under arrest for theft. He began to violently resist and was quite well-built, so Jess and I were both trying to stop him running off and get him in handcuffs; holding on desperately for the minute or so that it took for our uniformed colleagues to arrive and help us. He was successfully arrested and ultimately charged with handling stolen goods. The victim got her phone back and couldn't have been happier and more grateful to us. It's very rare for things to all fall into place exactly like this – the fact there were some plain clothes officers on duty at the time the lady came to the station and that we were successfully able to pull off the plan we'd made, so this was a good win for us. It was yet another abject demonstration of what can be achieved by a pro-active team.

***

Sometimes the sheer stupidity of an offender can be what makes things funny when you look back on it after the event, as was the case of a male who threatened me when I was working the Nottingham Goose Fair one year. My 'fixed-point' posting was the corner of Gregory Boulevard and Noel Street by the tram stops, which during the period of the Goose Fair is closed to traffic except residents. This is signposted quite clearly with numerous 'no right / left turn' signs, and big 'no entry' signs in the road. In spite of this, drivers would occasionally turn up there, so I would stop and speak to them and check their driving licence / insurance. One of the drivers I stopped was hostile to me straight away, shouting abuse and swearing at me barely before I'd even uttered a word. I tried to explain why I had stopped him but could hardly get a word in between his barrage of abuse. He then got out the car and walked round to me and when I asked for his driving licence he threw it at me, continuing his loud swearing. This was the middle of the afternoon on the Saturday of Goose Fair, so the area was packed with young families and children who could no doubt all hear his expletive-laden tirade. I gave him a warning about his language which he just shrugged at. As a result of the chap's attitude, I decided to give him a ticket for contravening the no-entry sign. I began explaining the ticket to him but he started walking off, leaving me with his driving licence. I shouted to him that he'd forgotten it, and he told me to bring it to him. I declined his offer and told him he could get it from Radford Road Police Station whenever he wanted to. He obviously didn't fancy doing that so he stormed back over, snatched it out my hand, got back in his car and drove off, wheel-spinning as he went.

Sometimes it's much easier to leave things be if they've resolved themselves. With him leaving the area there wouldn't be any more swearing and I could remain where I was and be available at the Goose Fair site for any more serious matters as well as community engagement. Policing is not always about prosecuting everyone for every minor infringement of the law; it's more often than not about exercising your powers of discretion. I felt that this was the best course of action in this instance - he would get three points on his licence for the traffic matter, there was no need to deal with him for public order offences now he'd left and so I thought no more of it.

That was until *an hour later* when I was happily talking to a family and their children, letting them try on my hat and pose for photos, when I noticed the same male from the car earlier came over to me, looked at my collar number, and walked off again. When

I finished speaking to the family he walked back over to me and without pausing for breath said "Just so you know, you've got my address and now I've got yours. I'm going to come and knock you out." He was also waving a bottle in my face, and due to how close he was I couldn't see if it was plastic or glass. I kept telling him to go away or he would be arrested, but his response was "make me". I *still* at this point was trying not to arrest him, due to needing to be available at the Goose Fair event. Instead I got out a dispersal notice ticket, which requires someone to leave an area for a set amount of time, and started writing it out. Suddenly he grabbed hold of my hand and tried to pull the pen out of it. There are limits to patience, tolerance and discretion, and this limit had finally been crossed with me. I felt I'd given this guy more of all those than he could ever have deserved. I took hold of his hand, spun him round, put handcuffs on him and arrested him for threatening behaviour and assaulting a police officer.

A van came and conveyed us to custody, where the Sergeant booking him in was gobsmacked as to the amount of chances that I had given the male to just go away, and that he'd then come back and specifically sought me out *an hour later* to threaten me! He was charged with assaulting a police officer and threatening behaviour, which he unsuccessfully challenged at court and received 80 hours community service, £260 in fines and costs, as well as the £60 and three penalty points on his licence for the original road traffic offence. All of which would have been completely avoidable had he just been reasonable.

If you are ever stopped by the police bear in mind that officers have extensive powers of discretion and will normally actively avoid creating extra work for themselves – be nice to them and they'll likely be nice to you! This is a lesson that many of the so-called 'justice warriors' or the like could really do with remembering. If the police stop you and you instantly shove a camera phone in their face, refuse to answer any questions and claim harassment or whatever, the officer is much more likely to respond in an entirely different manner than if you are polite. The psychological theory underpinning this is called 'Betari's Box' – my behaviour affects your behaviour and your behaviour affects my behaviour. If you're just *decent* to the officer and listen to what they say then you're far more likely to be on your way in next to no time with some words of advice. If you greet them with hostility then you're far more likely to be dealt with by the book and receive a more impactive outcome and be delayed considerably longer.

***

During my time covering the Lenton and Radford neighbourhood areas there was an ongoing series of violent-crime related offences where males linked to rival drugs gangs were attacking one another, often with weapons. I was acutely aware of the escalating tit-for-tat violence and made sure to know all of the persons suspected of being linked to the gangs, what vehicles they drove, and boned-up on methodology of how they dealt their drugs. As a result I would regularly stop vehicles in my area that were connected to them or try to identify new vehicles they were using, get information as to who was in those vehicles, identify anybody new associating with known suspects and feed this all back into police intelligence that would go to the Serious and Organised Crime team who were investigating the overall situation.

This led to me making several arrests myself for drugs supply offences and the Serious and Organised Crime team would often take over the investigations to link into their ongoing enquiry trying to get to those at the top. Once again the name of "PC Tom Andrews" became well-known amongst another criminal gang as an officer to be aware of. I got to know many of the main players too and formed grudging love / hate relationships with several of them where we always had a bit of banter whenever we encountered each another. This shows that it's entirely possible to be an effective police officer targeting those who need arresting and prosecuting, but also be grudgingly respected by those that you deal with. This respect led to several of them from opposing sides providing me with good intelligence against their rivals – the bonus for me was that both sides were doing it against each other.

During a trial following one particularly large-scale violent incident, I was at court at the same time for another case and got chatting to the officer dealing with the disorder investigation. I was told that all the violence that had taken place was between two rival drug supply gangs fighting for domination of a particularly lucrative drugs market in the city. Apparently the violence had started after three males had come out of prison following a conviction for drugs supply, where the police had located the drugs stash that they were supposed to be hiding. The trio now owed a significant sum of money for those drugs to their suppliers. The violence was between those who were looking out for the younger males and those from a rival gang who had supplied the drugs and who were trying to enforce the debt.

I put two and two together and realised that the original incident being referred to was the stop my colleague and I had made a few years before where we had recovered the MDMA from the car boot! This to me was an abject demonstration of the law of unintended consequences and chaos theory – every action has an unquantifiable outcome. Us doing our job those years previously had resulted in numerous people being assaulted and communities affected by large scale disorder incidents taking place on their doorsteps. It was difficult for me to process that one single action had caused all these consequences. It didn't deter me from continuing to be proactive though as I couldn't be responsible for other people's poor decisions. I couldn't not arrest drug dealers in case they sustained retribution from those higher up their pecking order. To become involved in that world was a decision they had made. It did mean though that every time I arrested a suspected drug dealer in future I would make a concerted plea to them as to whether there would be any fall-out on them as a result of losing the drugs. Especially those who were vulnerable. This could at least allow us to try and put safeguarding measures in place if they spoke to us.

The lure of drug dealing can be very appealing to a sector of disenfranchised young people who see the apparently glamourous lifestyles of those higher up the pecking order. To reach that level though, where they can afford the fancy cars, designer clothes and bottles of champagne, they have to navigate a very turbulent course where nearly everyone is out to get them. Any mistakes are punished either by the police and courts, rival drug dealers from competing gangs, or even their own gang members higher up the chain. Only very few ever reach a level where they are unlikely to get their hands dirty on a day-to-day basis and even then the police can still catch them. It only takes one stroke of luck for the police and those involved can lose years of their lives in prison. It's also fraught with risk of violence from your rivals and carries a very high risk of serious injury or even death – as evidenced by the current spate of stabbings and shootings of young people across the nation's cities. The lower and middle echelons of gang life are spent living in squalid flats, working all hours every day, constantly looking over your shoulder for rivals and the police and getting next to no reward for the effort. The reality is completely different to the illusion shown by the lucky few who make it to the higher levels, normally only briefly. The concept is explored brilliantly and very simply in a chapter of the book *Freakonomics* by Stephen Dubner and Steven Levitt and is well worth a read for even only casual readers.

***

Another particularly nasty violent incident during my time as a beat manager was the tragic killing of Aqib Mazhar in Forest Fields in Radford in 2016, who was stabbed in the back and died as a result. Five males have been convicted of manslaughter in relation to the killing, and three of those were well known to me prior to this incident. In probably the most momentous single action of my career I arrested two of them on suspicion of the murder at the same time.

The murder had shocked the community and several suspects were identified very quickly by the investigation team. Clearly anticipating the police discovering their identities and involvement a couple of the suspects who were related to each other went into hiding for a time. Early enquiries to locate them had proven unsuccessful and their details were circulated on police briefing systems as being wanted. I had met Mohammed Qasim and Qamran Ahmed numerous times during my service and was quite familiar with them – it's important to clarify here that police officers meet many people in the course of their duties for various reasons, a great percentage of whom have committed no criminal offences.

I'd just come on duty on an afternoon shift a week or so after the murder and was sorting out my admin at the station before I headed out on patrol. I saw a message flag up on the command-and-control system saying that Qamran Ahmed was at the front counter to see an officer. I immediately recognised the name and grabbed the only other person in the station at that time who was a council warden I got on well with. I went down to the front counter with the warden and sure enough there was Ahmed – and I immediately recognised that he was also with Mohammed Qasim.

They obviously knew what was going to happen and had apparently decided to hand themselves in after sorting their affairs out in the preceding days. I took both into a side room and said the immortal words:

"I am arresting you both on suspicion of the murder of Aqib Mazhar in Forest Fields last week."

I don't think there are many officers anywhere in the country who can boast that they have said "I am arresting you *both* on suspicion of murder...". It's rare enough to make an arrest for murder of one person during your entire career, let alone two simultaneously.

I took them to custody with some other officers who travelled back to the station to assist with transport. I was met there by detectives from the Major Crime Unit. The officer recognised me, as this was not the first murder arrest I had made and he'd worked with me following the previous one as well. He asked me "how many murder arrests have you got now?" and it turned out I had actually arrested more alleged murderers (three) than he had – on the homicide unit! The pair were ultimately convicted of manslaughter as it was established that they had not delivered the fatal blow,

Ahmed receiving seven years, and Qasim nine years and eleven months.

The previous murder I'd dealt with was horrific and probably one of the most seminal moments of my career in terms of my involvement in it. The incident itself was later described to the press after the trial had concluded by the experienced Senior Investigating Officer leading the investigation as "one of the most barbaric murders I have ever investigated".

It was just another average afternoon shift and I was bimbling about on patrol of my area, when a call came over the radio that the fire service were attending reports of a house fire with people apparently still in the property. Police will always attend these types of calls with the fire brigade to help with crowd control, road closures, as well as to conduct initial investigations to ascertain if there was any deliberate attempt to harm the people in the address. The location was given as Derby Grove in Lenton which was on my area, so I volunteered to attend. I drove to the Derby Road end of the street to put on a road closure so as to give the fire service a safe and sterile working area. Another colleague went to the Ilkeston Road end and other officers began travelling to the scene. As I arrived at the junction of Derby Grove and Derby Road I saw that the fire brigade had tapped a hydrant in the middle of the very busy Derby Road. I parked my police van next to it and began to put some cones out to stop cars hitting the hose that was coming out the ground in the middle of the carriageway.

As I was busy doing this a man in an orange t-shirt came up to me:

"Excuse me, excuse me"

"Sorry mate, I'm just a little busy now"

"No, I need to talk to you"

"If you just wait over there, I'll talk you in a minute" I said, pointing over at the pavement.

Then came words that will stay with me forever:

"No, I'm the one you're looking for. I am the guilty party. I set him and my house on fire."

This made me instantly stop what I was doing, almost do a double-take at him, before realising the gravity of what he'd just told me. I immediately took hold of him and as I got close I could smell petrol strongly emanating from his clothes. I got handcuffs on him and put him straight into the back of the van. At that point I only had limited information about what was actually happening, so to detain him and stop him leaving I said to him "I am arresting you on suspicion of arson with intent to endanger life". As he sat in the back of my van I got my pocket note book out and wrote in it exactly what he had just said to me. He was handcuffed to the front and best practice states that you should offer any 'significant statements' made by a suspect for them to sign after you write them down. I offered this written statement to the man who sure enough signed to acknowledge that he had just confessed the offence to me. Fans of the film *Hot Fuzz* will recognise that at this time my pocket book really was the most important piece of police equipment.

As more information came in over the radio it became apparent that there was a man in the address who had been engulfed by the flames. My colleague who'd gone to the other end of the road nearest to the address in question had gone into the house with the firefighters and paramedics and had come across this man, who was incredibly still alive. The nature of the updates I was getting over the radio were incredibly distressing with regards to this man's condition to the extent I won't relay them here. The ambulance crew apparently couldn't even really attempt any medical interventions with him, so severe were his burns. They literally loaded him into the ambulance and conveyed him, with my colleague driving the ambulance so they could both tend to him in the back, to the hospital for advanced help and treatment. Based on these updates I said to the man I had arrested, who by now had given me his name, Sekou Soumare, that he was further under arrest for attempted murder. The victim was still alive at this point but he had suffered 97% burns. I took Soumare to custody where I was met by the same detective as above from the Major Crimes Unit, which was where he recognised me from that later occasion. He helped me book Soumare into custody and took over from me. It wasn't until a few hours later that I had confirmation that the victim, Christopher Bonnick, had sadly died from his horrific, un-survivable injuries.

It later emerged after his interviews and the investigation that the victim was Soumare's landlord and the pair had had a disagreement over rent. Soumare had invited Bonnick to the address and there pretended to make amends and offered him drinks. He kept plying Bonnick with drink until he was paralytically drunk and then laid him down on an old mattress. He then put another mattress on top, covered him in petrol and set light to him before walking out the address and calling the fire brigade himself. He was set to plead not guilty by means of mental health issues, but changed this to guilty shortly before the trial was due to begin. He was sentenced to life with a minimum of 26 years. Definitely the biggest sentence anyone has received that I arrested. To act so callously and with so little regard for human life is something absolutely beyond me.

Other than the words of the confession he blurted out at me, the thing that stayed with me most from this was the overwhelming sense of waste. A waste of two precious human lives over something so trivial as rent arrears. I vividly remember the thought entering my head from nowhere as I was arresting Soumare and putting him into the back of my police van, that this was quite possibly the last moment of freedom he would experience. Closing of the van door felt really odd, doubling as a physical and metaphorical act – his last glimpse of the outside world. Considering the numbers of people I had arrested in my career previously, I'd always known they would only be deprived their liberty for a short time; this one I knew was different.

***

Police officers don't just deal with other people being assaulted, it often happens to them as well. One of the most memorable times I was attacked resulted once again from conducting pro-active patrols, this time using the force's Automatic Number Plate Recognition (ANPR) system on the then new 3G enabled laptops. The system alerted me to a vehicle very near to my location that had a marker on for possibly being involved in drug supply. I found the car a minute or so later and followed it whilst conducting checks via the radio. As I was waiting for the results it stopped of its own accord on a quiet residential street, all four doors opened simultaneously and the occupants did what is known in policing circles as 'starburst' – running off in different directions. In situations like this the driver is always the primary focus as they are the one that can be most definitively linked to anything found in the car as well as any possible driving offences. I gave chase whilst

122

updating on the radio what was happening. He ran straight up to the door of a house and began knocking on it loudly. I ran up the pathway behind him just as the door opened and he barged past the occupant and ran straight in, down the hallway to the kitchen at the back of the house. I followed him in and managed to grab hold of his arm. He spun himself round quickly, throwing me past him and causing me to slam into an upright fridge-freezer that was in front of us. He sprinted back towards the front door with me once again in pursuit. Having been thrown into a fridge and with the chap clearly intent on getting away, I pressed my radio emergency button to get more officers travelling to me and so I could have the open mic and not worry about having to use a hand to press the talk button. I managed to partially rugby tackle the driver as he was going through the door which knocked him off his feet, allowed me to catch up with him and to body-check him into the boundary wall at the front of the garden. I then managed to get handcuffs on him and arrested him for assaulting an officer, failing to stop for police and police obstruction. The other officers coming to my assistance managed to locate and detain one of the other passengers who'd run off and unfortunately for him was quite distinctive.

After securing our arrests in custody, the value of local policing intelligence generated by PCSO's and their worth to the policing model was proved to me when one of the PCSO's on the team told me she knew of the man I'd arrested. In custody he'd given an address that was his family home, but he clearly didn't live there. Helen the PCSO told me that she'd received some information that the chap had regularly been seen coming and going from a flat in her neighbourhood area. Based on this information we went to this flat and tried the key the male had in his possession in the door and it worked to unlock it! After getting the relevant search authority a search of the flat uncovered a significant quantity of class A drugs. The chap was dealt with the following morning and charged with numerous offences including possession with intent to supply class A drugs, the assault on me and driving offences. He received a hefty custodial sentence, once again proving both the benefits of pro-active policing and good community relations to obtain useful intelligence. I later received my second Divisional Commander's commendation for my tenacity in this incident, after being nominated by a colleague.

I was assaulted again one evening in 2015. Coincidentally only that very day I had been issued one of the force's brand new body-cams or body worn video cameras. These had only been introduced the month or so before and were being highlighted by the force on their external communications. I passionately believed in the benefits of them in preventing spurious complaints, deterring people from assaulting officers and providing crucial fairly indisputable evidence at court. On this first day with it I'd been sent to a report of some anti-social behaviour in a fast-food takeaway in Lenton, where a man was refusing to leave. I was on my own but was fairly confident that I could deal with the situation, so declined when the dispatcher asked if I wanted any further units to assist.

When I got there I was confronted by a chap who was accusing one of the takeaway staff members of being the Messiah come again and then berating him for being a false prophet. He refused to leave when the takeaway staff asked him and when I asked him. It didn't take a genius to work out that he was likely experiencing some form of mental health episode, but he was still fully aware of where he was and checks on his name suggested he only lived nearby. I asked what would get him to leave and he replied that if the Lord asked him to leave then he would do, gesturing towards the staff member he'd been talking to. I suggested to that staff member to ask the man to leave, which he did and the chap duly left. I followed him out to make sure he left the area and the man happily began walking up the road back towards his home address. Suddenly, completely out of nowhere he turned round and ran straight at me, shouting something about "the devil", got his hand around my neck and was strangling me before I could realise what was going on.

All the self-defence training in the world can't take away that element of surprise and fear when someone unexpectedly grabs you around the neck. After the split second it took me to process it and register what was happening though, survival instinct and training-induced muscle-memory took over. I immediately began hitting down on the crook of his arm to try and break his grip but due to the height of it I couldn't get enough power to dislodge him. I was able to hit the emergency button on my radio, one of only three times I've ever done so, then grabbed for my CS incapacitant spray, managing to aim it directly into the man's face. This had the desired effect and he immediately let go of my neck and grabbed his eyes as the irritant caused them to sting and water. CS is very nasty stuff, especially sprayed directly at your face as a liquid, and having used it before I knew it wouldn't be long before I too got its effects through cross-contamination. I managed to take advantage of the male's disorientation and with the incredible assistance of a passing cyclist who literally jumped off his bike, abandoned it in the middle of the road and came to my aid, I managed to get the male to the floor and in handcuffs.

The little orange button gets officers travelling from everywhere to your aid and it was only a minute or two before colleagues started arriving. Some officers came in a large van and helped me get the male into the prisoner cage in the back. By this time the CS was starting to take its toll on me and I was struggling to breathe and keep my eyes open. I managed to get the passer-by's details (and later successfully recommended him for a police commendation for helping me) and then took the arrested male to custody. CS is made worse by water as it washes the little crystals further into the skin. Instead, the best way of getting it off is by blowing it off. Therefore on the journey to custody I had my head hanging out the window of the van – like a dog – but the temporary effect that has is to blow the CS more into your eyes and face before blowing it off. Travelling at higher speeds on blue lights made it even worse and there were points on the journey in where I was physically unable to breathe! It truly is horrible stuff, and for days after being contaminated with it, it's impossible to wash yourself – or even sweat – without it stinging again as the crystals are dislodged and scrubbed in with the water.

The chap who strangled me was sectioned to a mental health facility the following day after an assessment of his faculties, so I declined to press charges against him. It's hardly fair, if he wasn't of sound mind, to prosecute him for something that he was not likely consciously doing. During the whole incident though I'd had my new body-worn video (BWV) camera on and it captured the entire thing perfectly. Any assault on a cop is flagged up at the following morning's senior officer's briefing which was attended by the project lead for the BWV programme. He got in touch with me, firstly to check I was OK, but also to see if I had caught it on camera, which of course I had. After showing him the footage he asked to use it in a media release, showing the benefits of the system. I was more than happy with this as I felt I had acted very reasonably in it, but made sure to make the communications team aware that the male had not been prosecuted and was suffering from a mental health crisis at the time. They ensured that his face was blanked out in the footage which appeared on the local BBC and ITV evening news broadcasts, as well as in the local paper and covered on the local radio. I gave interviews to all the media outlets explaining the circumstances and how I felt. It was not long later that the Chief Constable signed up to a national pledge relating to assaults on officers and as a result of that video I was again asked to be the face of officers on the ground who had been assaulted, appearing in the local paper and force social media again.

Both these assaults occurred when I was single-crewed – deployed on my own. This is predominantly the daily reality of a neighbourhood officer, being on your own, but is becoming increasingly common for response and other front-line officers too. If you're only expecting to deal with low-level neighbourhood issues, then it's not such a problem, but for those expecting to deal with more violent incidents – domestics, fights, organised criminals etc – then it can be dangerous. This is sadly another impact of Austerity and the need to "do more with less" by spreading resources thinner. The inevitable consequence is that officers on their own are more likely to be assaulted as they present an easier target to those who fancy their chances. It's only anecdotal evidence, but the vast majority of times I was assaulted I was on my own. Later, on the Knife Crime Team, when dealing with some really nasty individuals, I was rarely assaulted; but on that team stops were always conducted with at least two officers, and more joining very soon after.

During my career, other than the assaults mentioned, I have also been threatened with an iron bar; had someone brandish a hot clothing iron at me; pushed, pulled and punched more times than I can remember; had vehicles intentionally driven at me and had people tell me that they were going to find me outside of work and do unspeakable things to my family and me. I consider myself one of the lucky ones though. I've never been seriously injured. I know colleagues who've had bones broken; one of which was on a bank holiday shift where there was minimum staffing on. She was sent single-crewed to a domestic where the violent offender ended up fighting with her. She was in Lenton, and her urgent request for back-up resulted in just a single other unit being available to travel to help – from Eastwood.

Other colleagues have been attacked with weapons, and I was also on duty to hear over the radio a colleague get stabbed. That incident provoked a significant reaction, and every man and quite literally a couple of their (police) dogs went to that. The offender, a young person who was attending a youth intervention meeting, fell out with one of the other attendees and drew a knife he'd had on him, to threaten the other young man with. These were kids with no sense of mortality or consequence.

The officer, who was in plain clothes helping to facilitate the meeting, stepped in to speak with the knife-man. He got slashed for his troubles as the offender made a frantic bid for freedom. He made it to the other side of town before the thin blue net caught him. I don't know what happened to the youth, but the officer made a reasonably full recovery – from the physical injuries anyway. Other officers are less lucky, such as the one who was chasing a suspect, was pushed by the suspect and went over on his ankle, snapping several of the tendons and breaking some of the bones. He was never able to work on the front line again. Others have come up against cage fighters experiencing the effects of alcohol and / or cocaine binges and quite literally been fighting for their lives. Luckily back-up was not far away on that occasion either and the effective application of CS gave just enough time for the officer to get out the headlock that was rendering him unconscious before others could all pile on.

No-one expects policing to be a safe profession, but there seems to be an ever-increasing casualness to the use of violence against the police. Both by those physically doing it, and the encouragement – active or passive by filming it and not helping the officers – seems to be growing. Thankfully the government are finally taking action thanks to a prolonged campaign by the Police Federation, and sentences for those convicted of assaulting officers have (in theory) been doubled. In reality, some sentences handed down by the judiciary are still atrocious, and you have to wonder whether they would feel happy if the same sentence were handed to someone who attacked a family member of theirs. I regularly see stories of judges sentencing people who insult them in their court rooms to custodial sentences, whilst those who assault police officers get low level fines or community punishment. Hopefully things will improve with time.

***

Social media really took off during my time as a beat manager, especially for the police. Initially the force set up a single force-wide Twitter and Facebook page, but quickly realised the value in neighbourhood officers being able to directly update their communities who could follow them on the relevant platforms for specific local updates. Already being on reasonably good terms with the communications team I was asked to see if I wanted to trial one of the new accounts and so was granted access to a Twitter account covering Radford. This proved to be a big success as I was able to quickly provide updates about road closures following accidents and tag in the local news outlets and traffic and travel news sites. I could highlight good news stories and put out appeals for information, as well as just provide general updates about my daily activities. I soon got quite a number of followers including local news outlets. This meant that I began to appear in the paper quite regularly in short news stories as they would get the information for free from my Twitter account – much to the amusement of my colleagues who felt I was courting the limelight!

Such news stories included the time where a special constable and I were approached by a woman concerned for her neighbour who she hadn't seen for a couple of days which was really out of character. She couldn't get any answer to knocking her door or ringing the lady's phone. The lady of concern had mobility issues so couldn't go out on her own and the concerned neighbour normally saw her at least every other day to check she was OK. This set many alarm bells ringing, and after checks confirmed the lady in question wasn't in the hospital, we decided to put the door in. We entered the address and found the lady in the upstairs bedroom collapsed on the floor, alive but very tired. She'd fallen out the bed apparently two days before and been unable to get up or move to reach the phone to call for help. We hastily called an ambulance which took the lady to hospital where she made a full recovery. The special constable and I visited her at home a few days later when he was next back on duty to make sure she was OK. I am firmly convinced that the two of us and the concerned neighbour saved the woman's life that day, as from her condition I don't think she would have survived much longer. I put out a Tweet to this effect and the paper picked it up and ran a story about it.

Sometimes the direct communications links to other people via social media went wrong, and on one occasion I accused the editor of the local newspaper who I followed on Twitter of taking a picture on her phone whilst driving. It turned out she had been sat in the back seat taking the picture and a prompt apology to her thankfully resolved the issue. It was certainly a learning point for me though about the pitfalls of social media.

My success on Twitter meant that after a while when the force decided to set up local neighbourhood Facebook pages, I was asked to again be one of the first to trial this. It was an instant success through being able to publish longer, more in-depth explanations of our actions and appeals, as well as more people using Facebook and therefore being able to communicate to a wider audience. Such was its success that the force wanted to run a story to promote the new local Facebook pages to a wider audience and once again I was asked to be the face of this. The *Nottingham Post* photographer came and took a very imposing picture of me outside Canning Circus Police Station that was to be used by them on many future occasions whenever they ran a story featuring me. It also became a source of many memes created by my colleagues, especially one who jokingly often told me that being a beat manager consisted entirely of wearing slippers, hugging babies and eating Dundee cake.

***

My time as a beat manager also saw me achieve some of the proudest moments of my policing career, on two occasions where I was selected to represent the force at some really significant moments.

My interactions with the force communications team were not limited to my social media presence, but a colleague and I also used to help them as points of contact for various historical related enquiries that they received from time to time. This stemmed from where Rob and I had been approached by the Deputy Chief Constable at the time, Sue Fish, and the Women's Network within the force, to help celebrate the 100-year anniversary of women in policing, which took place in 2015. We were asked to compile something to demonstrate how the role of women within the police had developed throughout the century and given pretty much free reign as to how we went about this. Rob took the lead on it and I helped him out wherever possible. We'd been chosen due to our ongoing passion for preserving and sharing the force's history which had gained the notice of the communications team and senior officers. Working with a Superintendent who was the head of the Women's Network, we settled on producing a booklet detailing the lives of various female police officers over the preceding century. Accompanying this was a celebration evening where we compiled a film featuring short interviews with several of the women featured in the booklet who told us their stories, as well as current female police officers in various roles across the force.

This project was incredibly successful and a newspaper appeal for former policewomen resulted in us getting several retired officers. It was a fantastic experience visiting and interviewing them all, and they couldn't have been keener to share their stories. The presentation evening went spectacularly, with all our interviewees and their families attending and we had managed to source lots of old policing equipment, as well as photos and keepsakes supplied by some of our subjects.

Partly due to our involvement in this, but also due to Rob's regular organising of the force's annual Remembrance Day events, in 2016 we were approached by the communications team for something truly special. Every year each police force in the UK is required to send one officer to be part of the Civilian Services Contingent at the national Remembrance Parade event at the Cenotaph in London. The five East Midlands forces had combined and decided to send five officers from one force on a rolling five-year basis. 2016 was Nottinghamshire Police's turn, so Rob and I were contacted and asked if we would like to represent the force.

Of course we said yes. We were asked to nominate three like-minded colleagues which we duly did and the five of us travelled down to London the night before the Festival of Remembrance. We were put up in a hotel and then had an evening being briefed on our role and the expectations of us by the drill instructor.

The following morning was a very early start to clear security and enter the sterile area required due to the presence of Her Royal Highness the Queen and other dignitaries. We then spent several hours of drill practice near to Whitehall, before marching at the designated time to our place at the side of the road near the Cenotaph. We then stood for several hours at ease with the very specific instruction not to move. Trying to stand absolutely still for a period of around two hours is quite a challenge, as inevitably parts of your body start itching and aching. The overwhelming sense of pride and desire not to be the one caught on national TV looking all around them made sure that I did it though! Come the stroke of 11:00 we were called to attention and bowed our heads until the cannons on Horse Guards Parade and the sounds of the Last Post brought us out of our revelry. I saw nothing of the Queen or any other dignitaries, except the former Prime Minster David Cameron but had an incredible view of the veterans' march-past and did make a brief appearance on the TV, when I watched it back later. I also posed for photos in my dress uniform in front of 10 Downing Street and in the Foreign and Commonwealth Office where we were de-briefed after the event. It was also the last year that the Queen attended in person, due to her advancing years and ailing health. Nothing can put into words the immense pride I felt at being able to represent my country, the police service as a whole and Nottinghamshire Police specifically in this way. Every year on Remembrance Day, my mind goes back to that crisp sunny November Sunday in 2016.

I'd also had my third brush with Royalty only a few weeks prior to attending Remembrance Day in London, when His Royal Highness Prince Harry came to Nottingham. As part of the visit he officially opened the new Central Police Station at Byron House on Maid Marion Way. This was a formal event with press photo ops and planned activities for the Prince in the station. Rob and I were again asked to be part of the event, given our knowledge of protocols and our reliability and willingness to help the communications team and appear in the media. They knew we could be relied upon to be smart and presentable.

Rob and some of our other neighbourhood team colleagues were asked to be part of an officer's start-of shift briefing which Prince Harry would sit in on. I was instead privileged to be asked to form the guard of honour, with a council warden (with whom the police shared the building) on the front door of the station. I was requested to be in full tunic and helmet and stood beside the main door of the police station, opening it for the Prince.

I once again made the local news bulletins and the photographer from the force communications team took a couple of pictures for me on her own camera as Prince Harry was leaving. This included a spectacular one where he looks like he's about to come and embrace me as a long lost friend! The three-week period of this and the Remembrance Sunday Parade was a very surreal time for me at work.

The new station was opened sadly as a result of the closure of both Canning Circus and the old Central police stations. I had been on an afternoon shift at Canning Circus on the last day it was an operational police station. Having arrested someone quite late on in the shift I was two hours late off, meaning that I was the last operational officer to leave Canning Circus police station. Any officer who has ever worked at 'Canning on the Hill' as it was affectionately known doesn't have a bad word to say about it; its size and internal layout being ideal for close co-operation between different teams and intelligence sharing. Its closure was sadly as a result of austerity cuts, which had also seen the decimation of the neighbourhood team. I really enjoyed being a beat manager and the freedom that it brought to manage my own workload, but in mid-2016 I was offered an attachment opportunity that I couldn't turn down.

Knife Crime

I thought you were supposed to find knives, not drugs?

In mid-2016 Nottinghamshire Police decided to take action to try and stem the rising tide of knife-enabled crime and introduced the only dedicated Knife Crime Team outside of the Metropolitan Police's 'Serious Violence Reduction Unit'. The team had just one task – target those who might seek to use weapons, in an attempt to reduce knife-enabled crime and serious violence. Unfortunately, lacking the resources of the Met, the team consisted of just six officers and a Sergeant. The team was also initially only temporary in order to monitor its progress and see how it performed, so it was therefore staffed by officers on temporary attachment. The Sergeant who established the team deliberately sought out officers with proven pro-active experience to help formulate the team's tactics and also pass on those skills to a new generation of officers who might come through.

After the team had been running for three months, a new round of attachments was due and I was approached by my Inspector who was required to send one of his officers. The three experienced longer-serving team members were to remain and somehow I'd come to their attention and they'd recommended to their Sergeant to ask my Inspector if he could release me. Luckily he'd agreed and I didn't flinch when I was asked if I wanted the opportunity – this role was exactly what I'd wanted to do throughout my career. In September of that year I joined the Knife Crime Team, supposedly on a three-month attachment.

The level of ability in pro-active policing displayed by the three experienced team members was incredible. One of them especially seemed to have some kind of supernatural ability for finding baddies, and was most certainly a super-recogniser – someone who has an ability to remember almost limitless numbers of faces and names. Because we were only a temporary team we had only limited access to vehicles and we had to adapt our tactics to fit that accordingly. We would have an unmarked car and a marked car if we could get our hands on one. Our deployments were to all different areas of the city for a couple of weeks at a time, on a threat, harm and risk basis around the likelihood of knife crime in that area. We'd often be joined by a local officer as a spotter who knew the local faces and the recent intelligence. The plain car would then observe anyone who we saw out and about who fit the criteria of having been involved in knife-related incidents, linked to gang crime, or whom there was intelligence on suggesting they carried knives. After watching a short time either the marked car would stop them, or if we didn't have one we would get out the plain car and stop them.

The skills of the team meant that we were regularly making successful stops and there was rarely a shift went by that we didn't have a positive stop and search and most months our positive outcome rate (times when we found something illegal on the person we were searching) was around 70 – 80%. For context the national average at that time was around 30%. These were also significant results, not just simple possessions of cannabis offences. We were finding supply quantities of drugs probably almost every other day and knives once or twice a week. I won't pretend that I was responsible for a significant number of these, certainly not initially, but as time went on and I learned some of the skills I found a more equal share of the jobs.

The officers on the team were passionate about what we were doing, locking up baddies. There weren't many shifts went by without us being several hours late off after making an arrest and then having to conduct house searches, interviews and getting our detainee remanded to court the following morning. No-one moaned, complained or begrudged it, and if someone needed to be off on time for some reason, the team would take it in turns to stay and deal. It really was a golden time. It was also the first time that I had policed anywhere outside of my existing comfort zone of Lenton, Radford, Wollaton and the City Centre – going to places such as Bulwell, St Ann's and Broxtowe, and later even further afield into the county areas such as Sutton-In-Ashfield and Mansfield.

The only issue came with the constant office politics; both from some senior officers and colleagues in other departments – perhaps motivated by jealousy – that we regularly found drugs when we were "supposed to be a Knife Crime Team". I am firmly of the opinion that without the drugs issue there would be a significantly smaller knife crime problem. The vast majority of knife-enabled crimes can be linked back to drugs – whether that be the gang members using knives to settle disputes, expand territory or enforce debts; or the users robbing innocent victims with weapons to fund their habits. Therefore if you target the drugs you can take out the people who might be likely to use the knives before they get a chance to, and they're also more likely to be the ones carrying the knives.

It's also far easier to get the grounds to search someone for drugs than it is for knives. Firstly, cannabis smells. It's that simple. It largely gives you grounds to search someone on its own (the Independent Office of Police Conduct and College of Policing says that it's not sufficient grounds without anything else, but if you're talking to someone on their own, who stinks of cannabis, are you really not going to search them?). A lot of the public hate drugs as well and especially those who deal them, so will provide intelligence to the police or CrimeStoppers about people involved in drugs. Especially drug users who have either been ripped off or threatened by their dealer! It was also possible, especially in the plain car, to witness drug deals taking place when you know what to look for. None of these things have comparisons for knives. There would occasionally be intelligence for someone carrying a knife, or of people who had been involved in knife crime recently and then grounds could exist, but these occasions were few and far between.

There is also the benefit of how seriously court sentencing guidelines views drug supply offences; the starting point for supplying class A drugs for a first-time offender is a couple of years in prison. There aren't many other offences for which this is the case, including possession of a knife in public (only six months imprisonment for a second offence!) or serious violence. If you can get those people who are likely to be involved in knife crime sent to prison then they can't be a victim or an offender... Sadly some of our colleagues who should have known better couldn't see this connection, either through wilful or unconscious ignorance and we would often be questioned about our high number of drug investigations.

Perhaps my greatest early find after joining the team came one afternoon, when one of the team recognised a local street level drug dealer whom they had previously sent to prison but was now back out again. The man's behaviour and mannerisms were out of place so we observed him for a short time during which he went into a house and came back out only a short time later. Of itself this wasn't grounds to search him, but we decided to stop him after he went a short distance from the house and see what he was doing. As soon as my colleagues approached and identified themselves as officers he attempted to run off. A big bonus of being in plain clothes was that we were in trainers too and not the very heavy full police uniform and boots, so he was quickly detained. Running off from the police, coupled with the other background, meant there was definitely grounds to search him and my colleagues found several thousand pounds in cash secreted on him. For someone without a job he wasn't really able to explain where he got it from. This could only mean one thing and he was arrested for money laundering (possession of criminal property).

Having just seen him leave an address immediately prior to his arrest it gave us a power to enter and search that premises. Another colleague and I who'd remained outside the address just in case this was how the stop turned out, went to the address and knocked the door. A head came out of an upstairs window and the man was immediately recognised by my colleague, the super-recogniser, as being one of the suspected local gang members, and a higher-level member at that. He refused to answer the door, locked all the windows and tried to go out the back door – luckily another colleague had already got that possibility covered off and had the back garden covered. We got a couple more officers to join us and eventually put the door in with the big red key and secured the occupant downstairs along with the chap we'd already arrested. We then began searching the address to see if there was more cash, or if it was the proceeds from the sale of something illegal. We certainly weren't expecting what we did find.

I took an upstairs bedroom, where stuffed behind a wardrobe was a 'bag-for-life' carrier bag. I pulled it out and noticed it was quite heavy. Inside was another carrier bag, which I turned upside-down to let whatever was in it fall out and there was a loud 'thunk' on the bare wooden floorboards as a shiny silver revolver handgun fell onto the floor at my feet. "SARGE!" was my cry from upstairs to the Sergeant who was looking after the two detainees downstairs. I was joined by the Sergeant and one of my other colleagues to look at the gun after which I went down and arrested the pair for the possession of it.

We were soon joined by CID and scenes of crime officers as well as a specialist search team to do a comprehensive search of the address. The two males were taken to custody and CID took the investigation off us. A picture of the firearm got printed off and stuck on the wall of our office – a proud team tradition of putting a picture on the office wall of every weapon seized as a reminder of what we did and the benefits we brought. It also made a cracking visual impact to anyone who came into our office, including the Chief Constable, Police and Crime Commissioner and various TV and news reporters.

The gun turned out to be an old revolver, loaded with viable large calibre ammunition that would have done some very real damage to anyone shot with it, and was 'ready to go'. When I found out it was loaded and cocked, it really brought it home to me considering I had dropped it out the bag onto the floor at my feet – it could have apparently easily gone off and shot my foot off. The second man, the one who was in the address, was charged with possession of a firearm and ammunition and remanded to prison. His fingerprints were found on the external carrier bag and the investigation team found a YouTube drill music video of him rapping about owning a silver .44; but for reasons known only to them in their deliberation room, he was acquitted by the jury at trial.

I saw him a few weeks after he got out of jail following his not-guilty verdict and he recognised me, shouting to me "freedom tastes great!". As an officer you can't let this get to you, and the oft-repeated motto of all cops is "they all come again." And this particular individual did when he was arrested again a few years later in physical possession of another firearm. This time he did go to jail, for a whopping 24 years! Sadly I haven't seen him to ask how imprisonment tastes...

This was probably the most serious weapon that we found on the team, but it wasn't the only one. After we'd been operating successfully for six months and having removed in excess of 75 weapons from the street as well as countless drug suppliers, one senior officer decided that he wanted the three experienced team members back to their normal duties. He also wasn't prepared to send anyone else to replace them, citing diminishing staffing numbers on his teams. Losing half the strength of the team with protectionist bosses not wanting to release any of their staff to replace them meant that there was no alternative for it but to disband. This is really demonstrative of some of the old-school silo thinking typical in the police of old. It didn't matter that we had no doubt prevented numerous murders and serious assaults that would have taken entire CID team to investigate – a CID superintendent wanted his three detectives back. Our rest days came and we all said our farewells.

After six months of being able to undertake a role I loved, I prepared myself to go back to uniform and being a beat manager once again. The added irony here was that the team had been granted a special award at the force's annual awards ceremony in recognition of our Herculean efforts in arresting so many prolific offenders and taking so many weapons off the street. By the time we were informed of the award and invited to attend the ceremony to receive it from the Chief Constable, we'd also been told we were being disbanded. We all boycotted the awards ceremony as a result.

On those same set of rest days I received a call from my Inspector asking if I wanted to remain on a newly revamped Knife Crime Team! The Chief Constable had reportedly got wind that the team was being disbanded and was adamant that would not happen.

He directed that the team be kept and replacement officers found from elsewhere. For a couple of weeks it was just the Sergeant and me whilst we waited for the new officers to be released to join us, but we still made a few good arrests during that time. The team was then re-born with the Sergeant and me as the only surviving members from before, with four new officers joining us. One of these was Lee who'd helped me TPAC the mobility scooter, and who I'd worked with on response for several years.

As part of the re-launch we were also given exclusive use of two marked cars and managed to acquire some of the still fairly new mobile data-enabled laptops as well. The new team members were not as experienced in pro-active work, so we had to re-imagine our tactics especially with the extra use of the marked cars. I'd already had success with using the force's ANPR systems, so after a couple of weeks I introduced this idea to the team and took one of the computers out with me. We had barely been out five minutes when an alarm went off that a car with intelligence linking it to drugs and weapons was heading our way. Sure enough it appeared moments later and we got behind it, signalling it to stop. It carried on driving for a short distance before stopping, which always makes you a little suspicious. No sooner than it had eventually slowed to a stop than the driver got out and started running.

As the passenger, I was out like a flash and on his tail. Sadly for him, the driver was not built for running – to put it politely. He made it about 50 yards before he slowed and stopped, put his hands up and gave up. I quickly got him in handcuffs and searched him; the large bundle of wraps of powder that looked suspiciously like class A drugs that was in his 'man bag' gave me a bit of a clue as to why he'd run. There were also drugs in the car as well as several phones and scales, so both driver and passenger got arrested.

After lodging the pair at the custody suite, we went and did the house searches. Hidden in a big tub of sand in the garden shed at the passenger's house we found some 32 rounds of live ammunition for a handgun. At the driver's house a disassembled handgun was also found, although this later turned out not to be viable – only a replica. According to their phone messages, the pair had been drug dealing for quite some time around one of Nottingham's outlying villages. The driver was known to apparently be quite tough with people who crossed him, but this certainly wasn't my experience with him. The supposed 'hard man' broke down in tears when I booked him into custody, when it hit him that he was probably going to prison. It's often the case that people who are 'hard' on the street or in front of their mates, are often not so much when they're on their own faced with the consequences of their actions. The pair were convicted of numerous offences and sent to prison for several years.

This proved to the bosses the value of the ANPR system and was used as an example in several funding bids to acquire new kit for the team in terms of agile working devices and increased ANPR capabilities.

***

There was a fair share of funny moments on the Knife Crime Team as well, as with the rest of my other job roles in the police. In this case though it's certainly funnier in hindsight than it was at the time. I was crewed up with Lee when we saw a 'ropey' looking vehicle that piqued our interest. A quick check of it showed that it had no insurance – as good a reason as any for some initial questions, so we followed it intending to stop it in a safe place. Instead it pulled onto the driveway of a house. The car was not registered to that address, so we didn't think that it was the driver's house. As we got out the police car to go and speak to him, he got out his car very quickly and started heading towards a gate at the end of the drive. We asked him to stop and come and talk to us, but he ignored us, raising our suspicions significantly. He wasn't able to open the gate very quickly, so we caught up to him and started trying to explain why we'd stopped him and ask whether this was his house. He mumbled something about yes it was his house and that all his documents were inside. Just then he managed to open the gate, and backed towards the side door of the house. We didn't want him to go inside until we at least had some idea of who he was because we didn't know if it was his, or if he was trying to get into a stranger's house simply to get away from us. If it was his house and he went inside and didn't come back out, we wouldn't have a power to go in after him in these circumstances either, just for minor driving offences.

As he started to try and open the door, we took hold of him gently and began explaining that he needed to remain with us until we had finished our enquiries. Just as we got a grip of his arm though, he flailed it round wildly and ran to the bottom of the grassy garden. I say grassy. It may once have been grassy, now it was just muddy. It wasn't so much a case of running as sliding to the bottom of the garden, with the two of us trying to slide our way after him. He got to the waist-high fence at the bottom of the garden and tried jumping over it, but we managed to grab him before he could. Unfortunately with all the mud it was impossible to get any traction to create purchase for us to pull him down. It became a proper wrestling match with him trying to pull himself over this fence and the pair of us sliding around trying to stop him. To make matters worse, the longer we were there it became apparent that a large percentage of the sticky brown matter in the garden was not mud, but something else. There was a dog in the address – we could hear it barking – and it dawned on us that the owner just let it into the garden to do its business and didn't worry about picking up after it. A significant amount of the garden was covered in dog faeces and now a significant percentage of our clothing was too. The struggle became not about trying to get the man down to the floor to control him, but to try and keep on our feet so as to not end up covered in shit!

The tug of war wasn't getting us anywhere, so the suspect got a face full of CS from Lee. This affected us as much as it did him and made it extra difficult to restrain him. It did provide us with the small advantage we needed just to pin him up against the fence and await backup that we had requested as soon as we had started struggling with him. Once those officers arrived they were able to help us secure him properly with handcuffs and *very carefully* walk him back to the waiting police van – we certainly weren't putting him in a car to ruin the seats! As he was put in the van, some of the officers who had come to our aid searched the areas where he'd been. They discovered that underneath the male's car were two cling film balls, filled with little wraps of powder. That instantly explained his drastic desire to get away and it gave me great pleasure to further arrest him for possession with intent to supply class A drugs.

Lee and I took a very careful trip back to the police station, stinking to high heaven, and got changed. Our poo-covered clothes were bagged up and sealed! Mrs Andrews was not happy at my use of the washing machine that day for my dirty work clothes...

Evidence recovered from his phone showed that the man had just collected the drugs from someone higher in the supply chain and appeared likely to be intending to distribute them in the local area. It *had* been his house that he was trying to get into, where he lived with his wife and small children. A social services referral was made about the state of the address and the fact that the chap was apparently going to keep class A drugs there with the young children. The man was sent to prison for several years for the drug supply offences. It also turned out he had previously been deported from the country and had snuck back in again. He was deported for a second time following his prison term for this incident. This still didn't stop him, and in a sad reflection of the immigration system he popped up on intelligence briefings again a few years later as once again having snuck back into the country. I can't say I blame him to be honest though, as his wife and kids were here. Lee and I regularly look back and laugh about the time that we literally got covered in shit, but it definitely wasn't funny at the time.

***

I've already alluded to the fact that a large part of the role of the Knife Crime Team was conducting stop and searches. This is a very contentious tactic drawing strong criticism from certain sections of society, but we were confident in our use of it and achieved consistently high positive outcome rates. Some communities who are traditionally hostile to the use stop and search were actually complimentary of the team and the way we conducted them, and asked us to do more because they knew we were targeting the right people. There is a lot of attention given to supposed discrimination in stop and search – particularly towards Black, Asian and Minority Ethnic (BAME) communities. It is my unequivocal experience that the police are not discriminatory in their use of any powers – certainly not in the manner implied by the populist headlines. Yes the police discriminate in stop and search tactics. They would be foolish not to. But before this statement becomes misquoted, the discrimination takes all forms, and is based on the assessment of information from all sources – crime trends, recent intelligence and hotspots among other things. The police target stop and search appropriately. For example, only a tiny proportion of stop and searches are of women; an even smaller number of people aged over 65. But yet women make up just over 50% of the population and only account for 7% of stop and searches conducted between 1st September 2018 and 31st August 2019 – the last full year for which Nottinghamshire Police data is available and before the pandemic hit. Over 65's account for 21% of Nottinghamshire's population but yet stop and searches of people over the age of 35 (the highest the bandings go up to!) account for 26%. Some 46% of searches were of people aged 10 – 24 despite them making up only 23% of the population.[*] So the police are discriminatory, especially against young men, over say women or old people. But *should* the police be searching women and old people? Probably not, no, because data and intelligence indicate they are not likely to be involved in crime.

Sadly it is young people, and disproportionately young people from BAME communities, that information and experience shows are most likely to be involved in crime. Particularly those crimes where stop and search is likely to be an effective deterrent and detective tactic. This is fundamentally not the police's fault. Cops police society as it is, not a utopian ideal of society where everyone has equal opportunities in life. Until the historic imbalances that

---

[*] *Data from* www.police.uk *and*
https://www.nottinghamshireinsight.org.uk/research-areas/jsna/summaries-and-overviews/the-people-of-nottinghamshire-2017/ *as accessed Feb 2021*

mean poorer inner-city suburbs which are more prone to criminal activity are no longer disproportionately made up of those from BAME communities, this situation will continue. From my work in academic research around this since leaving the police, there are also key considerations around cultures of those communities too. One example is that male parents from Caribbean communities are statistically far less likely to remain in the household to help bring up their children and provide a stable male role model. Another is that some Indo-Pakistani cultures place significant value on outward displays of wealth, which can encourage younger generations into attempts to accumulate that visible display of wealth in perhaps nefarious ways. These statements are based on academic research into the subject, coupled with my own personal experience in a professional capacity. They are not by any means sweeping statements and true of *everyone* from those cultures. Far, *far* from it. It is merely indicative of a small percentage of those diverse communities and why research has shown that a significantly disproportionate percentage of young black males especially are drawn to criminal lifestyles. The same situations also lead to young white males being drawn to crime.

It is time to re-frame the situation and look at where blame should truly lie for this imbalance in opportunities for young disadvantaged groups and the resultant disproportionate involvement in criminality. Society as a whole is still stuck with a hangover from the colonial and Windrush eras, where some communities were marginalised and treated as second-class citizens, despite being in the UK at our request. Inequality still exists from this time period, and it is up to society as a whole to address this and fight for improvements in opportunities and access for all people. When 10% of households hold 43% of UK wealth, and the bottom 50% only have 9% of the money, something isn't right.* We must stop blaming the police for simply working in the society that exists. This is, in my opinion, the fault of politicians – who find an easy scapegoat in the police, to distract attention from their own economic policy failings, and inability to address these historic imbalances. Blame those who interact with the disadvantaged, rather than those who caused it. Sadly the media are all too happy to go along with this narrative, rather than critically analyse the situation, because it creates bolder headlines and sells copies; as well as perhaps exacting a form of revenge for police involvement in their affairs like the phone hacking scandal.

Thankfully the police and partner agencies are gradually moving towards a more educational approach and away from punitive for young people involved in crime. If they can be deterred from becoming further involved in criminality, then all the evidence shows that they have vastly improved life chances. I'm glad to say on the Knife Crime Team that we were part of this, on several occasions actively working with the Youth Offending Team to try and find employment for young people we stopped who it was evident were on the downward slope to more serious criminality. Some it worked for and we didn't see again; unfortunately it wasn't successful every time though.

Race and the disproportionality of the use of various police tactics (stop and search and use of force to name but a couple) against people of different backgrounds are such hot topics currently that I am hesitant to even consider those issues in this book for fear of backlash. I've done so though to try and emphasise why the police do disproportionately conduct stop and searches

---

* ONS data. Household total wealth in Great Britain: April 2018 to March 2020

against young black males – they form a disproportionate number of the tragic casualties at the hands of violent crime, and of those exploited by and sucked into criminal gangs. I am heartened though by an interview given by the Deputy Commissioner of the Metropolitan Police Sir Stephen House saying very similar things to the above. He is possibly the very first senior officer I am aware of to have publicly come out and said such things. Of course, this interview was only published in a local London newspaper, whilst national press once again led with police-bashing headlines about disproportionality.[*]

There is also a fascinating article written several years ago by a former key Home Office advisor about the truth behind so-called stop and search disproportionality. In summary it concludes that stop and search is nowhere near as disproportionate as it is made out to be. Certainly if you look at the figures *as a whole* it does appear to be, but if you focus on specific areas the figures are a lot less skewed. If you take Nottinghamshire as a whole for example, where the BAME residents make up only 4% of the population, so a BAME stop and search rate of anything over 4% looks disproportionate. In just the city area though, that figure jumps significantly to 35% of the population. Now it takes for more than one in three searches to be of BAME persons to appear disproportionate. If you focus down even further to a diverse area in the city such as St Ann's or Forest Fields, the percentage of residents from a BAME background jumps to 42 and 43% respectively.[†] Suddenly if nearly half of all searches in those areas are of BAME persons, this is consistent with the population as a whole. But when you extrapolate that back up again to the whole county, it only takes for a very small number of searches in those areas to start tipping the disproportionality figure over the 4% of the county as a whole.

Sadly areas such as St Ann's and Forest Fields are also where crime and intelligence data suggest that activities such as gang crime, drug dealing and the carrying of knives are more prevalent. If the police are expected to balance the figures back on a county-wide scale, the only really practical solution to this is to focus stop-and search operations (and the associated resources) on the sleepy villages and towns that don't have a large crime issue, but do have a predominantly white population. This is clearly a ludicrous option and would no doubt result in a rise in crime in the troubled areas that the officers were redeployed from, as well as send the positive outcome rate for searches plummeting through the floor. I am not suggesting that people in sleepy villages are not responsible for committing crimes, and especially not that white people are not responsible for crimes. Just that the specific socio-economic situations of those who happen to live in the poorer inner-city suburbs are more likely to be involved in criminality, and that at present, those areas comprise of a larger percentage of BAME residents.

The article in question appeared in *The Spectator* on 17th November 2018 and is titled 'The Stop and Search Race Myth'. It explains this phenomenon in slightly more detail but essentially concludes that on such a local level as individual neighbourhood areas, stop and search is negligibly disproportionate at best. But this did not sit in line with Theresa May and her war on the police during her time as Home Secretary, and as such this academic insightful look at the figures was swept under the carpet, in favour of the discrimination headline. This decision, and the war on stop and search by that same Home Secretary, has cost the lives of countless young boys as a result of the rise of knife crime, and countless more sucked into the gang lifestyle of drug dealing through a loss of the simple fear of being caught. This fear of being caught has similarly proven in academic research to be a big deterrent – bizarrely, significantly bigger than the fear of punishment. It has also caused untold issues for the police and set relations between them and the black community especially, back by a decade or more.

***

On occasion, some criminals don't want the police to find whatever contraband they might have with them, and go to extra measures to hide it in areas that the police don't normally check. I'll let you use your imaginations as to what dark recesses some folk will 'plug' items into to try and avoid their detection. The grounds required to strip search people are necessarily high – clearly the general public don't want the police to go around making people take all their clothes off, just to check they don't have a small amount of cannabis in their underwear. Often the grounds to require someone to bare all do exist and it's necessary to conduct full searches of a suspect. This is as unpleasant for the officers as it is the person being searched, and sometimes even more so.

I conducted dozens of strip searches, the majority of which were during my time on the KCT and there are a couple that really stand out for me as having been particularly unpleasant. On one occasion I'd arrested a male who we suspected had further drugs concealed about his person. The threshold for a strip search of someone already under arrest and in custody is slightly lower than for wanting to search a person stopped in the street. Custody staff need to ensure that the arrested person doesn't have anything secreted on them that they can use to harm themselves or the custody staff with. This prisoner was very reluctant to be strip searched when the custody Sergeant told him that's what was going to happen. As far as tell-tale signs go for having something secreted, his heightened reluctance to undergo the procedure was well up there. We took him to a cell and eventually negotiated him into starting the process. We got to his underwear when he just sat down and point-blank refused to take it off. After several minutes of coaxing he ultimately agreed to take them off, stood up and pulled them down. As his underwear fell the floor, so did a single small deal bag of cannabis. No-one goes to the effort of hiding just one small bag of cannabis in their bum-crack, so we told him to turn around and "widen his stance" (a polite way to say the otherwise quite suggestive "spread your legs!") to try and encourage the rest to fall out.

Instead of doing what we'd asked, the man, who was completely naked from the waist down, lunged straight at me and wrapped his arm around my neck. In less than half a second he'd got me into a head-lock. It was all I could do to drive him backwards, like a rugby scrum, onto the raised bed area in the cell which caused his knees to bend and him to collapse onto it. My colleague who was in the cell with me started shouting for assistance and came to my aid, punching the chap's arm in an attempt to make him release his grip. I was trying to get my hands between his arm and my neck as breathing quickly became more difficult. My colleague punching him might sound very aggressive and not 'police officer-like', but it is an approved use of force tactic to both distract the subject and to try and give a dead arm by stunning the nerves. If someone has their arm around someone else's neck, pretty much anything is fair game to get them off.

Luckily my colleague's shouts attracted the attention of a passing custody detention officer who hit the panic alarm. Every available officer in the custody suite came running into the cell to assist. With the extra officers arriving they managed to get the male to release his grip from my neck and pinned him to the floor. During the scuffle a large bag containing numerous individual smaller deal bags had fallen to the floor. Because I'd been the victim of the assault, my colleague was the lucky one who got to seize the 'ass drugs' – always a thrilling prospect to any police officer. The prisoner was later convicted of possession with intent to supply cannabis and assaulting a police officer.

On another occasion many years before, I'd detained a male under the Mental Health Act who'd been trying to harm himself. He'd also potentially committed criminal offences, so had been taken to custody rather than a hospital. When we'd got to custody the chap said that he was going to harm himself and told the Sergeant that he had razor blades on him. This meant that we had to strip search him to make sure that he didn't have anything on him that he could use to self-harm.

Unfortunately his mental health condition meant that he was unable to take much good care of himself and it was apparent that he hadn't washed in quite some time. As we were asking him to take different clothes off, most of them were very dirty. The most distressing part was when it came to taking his underwear off. He clearly struggled to wipe properly after having a poo, and his underwear was coated in faecal matter to the point it was almost crisp. Luckily there was a large stash of new spare clothes in custody, so we were able to provide him with clean clothing. He was never charged with any criminal offences and was found accommodation in a supported living premises, allowing him access to the help he clearly needed. Yet another person who no fault of their own was unable to properly care for themselves, but had fallen through the cracks. At least we were able to finally get him that help.

Another person we'd stopped on the Knife Crime Team was a male linked to drug supply who had warning on the intelligence systems for concealing items about his person. Due to the circumstances we'd stopped him in, we had a strip search authorised and took him back to the local police station. We went through the motions and got to him taking his underwear off. He told us he had no issues with being strip searched as he'd been to prison numerous times and was used to it because it happened regularly in there. Off came his underwear and he turned round and spread his legs. Visibly hanging down the inside of his thigh was a small strand of something like string. Initially I couldn't work out what it was and asked "what's that? Clearly it's not supposed to be there." The male felt inside his legs and without missing a beat said "oh, that's just toilet paper where I mustn't have wiped properly." He then tried to brush it away but it wouldn't and my eyes following it up his leg saw it clearly went into his anus. It was obvious that there was something up there that shouldn't be and I realised that the string hanging down was actually a thin strand of cling film. Police officers aren't allowed to try and retrieve items from intimate areas – there would be some pretty serious ethical and potentially medical concerns if that were the case. This meant we had to take the man to hospital and either have medical staff remove it or wait for it to come out naturally...

Unfortunately, because the chap knew the game was up, he became incredibly abusive and rude. Some criminals know how to play the system and waste cops' time if the police are going to take away theirs. His violent and abusive behaviour at the hospital meant that it required three of us to remain with him. He was in the main waiting area for the Emergency Department, continually swearing and being abusive towards us. There was very little that we could even do about it. Other than further arresting him for public order offences, we couldn't remove him because he needed the medical treatment to take out whatever was up his bum. We had to stay in the waiting room which was full of sick people, many of them elderly or young. This is one of the worst aspects of being a police officer. Sometimes you are just required to take abuse; and this was a real vitriolic tirade as he had nothing to lose – a conviction for a minor public order offence doesn't mean anything to a man who had dozens of previous convictions. We had to wait some four hours with him behaving like this whilst we waited for an X-ray. Again it was a case that the medical staff didn't want to fast track a man who was being so abusive, simply for that reason. It would set a very bad precedent for anyone visiting in future that if you kick off you get seen quicker.

The abusive man eventually agreed to go into a cubicle with a medical professional and retrieve the item himself. They emerged a few minutes later and the detainee handed over a finger phone wrapped in layers of cling film. A finger phone is exactly as it is described – a phone about the size of a finger. I can't think of many reasons why anyone would want a phone this small, other than the one that we're concerned with here. There weren't even any drugs – it was only the phone, which wasn't even illegal. If he'd simply produced it to us all those hours ago he would have been free to go on his way!

The chap told us that this was his 'prison phone' that he had kept with him – or rather *in* him – for 4 years, and it had been to prison with him twice. The fact that phones are even manufactured in this shape and size to begin with shows that there must be a reasonable demand for them, making this chap far from unique. This just goes to show the level that some criminals are prepared to go to, to improve their time in prison.

***

During my time on the Knife Crime Team it was not uncommon for vehicles to fail to stop for us when signalled to do so. The types of people we were looking for often drove around in pool cars which are cheap unregistered and uninsured vehicles that are used by organised criminals to get around in so that they can't be traced. If they are transporting contraband – drugs or weapons etc – then they have nothing to lose by trying to get away. If they get caught they'd only be facing some additional driving charges that wouldn't really add much to their sentence if they're caught with a load of drugs. As a result of this, eventually all the team got training in pursuit driving and the use of Stinger tyre deflation devices. This now meant that if a vehicle failed to stop for us we could pursue it until traffic or armed response officers could get to us and take over, and we could assist by trying to stop it with the Stingers.

I took part in several pursuits which are probably one of the most terrifying and adrenaline-fuelled aspects of policing. You're trying to keep up with someone who is determined to get away and therefore driving at excess speed, with little concern for other road users and pedestrians. At the same time you need to maintain your own driving standards and provide a clear and calm commentary to allow other officers to get to your location and help stop the fleeing driver.

I once pursued a vehicle down Derby Road out of the city centre through Lenton in the late evening. There was little other traffic on the road, meaning we got up to quite high speeds. As we approached QMC Island the fleeing driver slightly misjudged a corner and smashed into the back of another car that was slowing for the roundabout. The offending car went up almost vertically into the air on its front bumper, pirouetted round 180º and landed on its wheels, facing back towards me. Apparently un-phased, even with the front bumper hanging off, the driver managed to floor it, turn the car round again and continue off the way he'd been heading to begin with. Given the extreme manner of driving and the serious-looking collision with an innocent motorist, I was left with little choice but to abort the pursuit. I went to check that the occupants of the car that had been hit were OK and take their details. Thankfully they were all fine and there was comparatively little damage to their car as well. The person responsible frustratingly managed to get away on this occasion, but the safety of the public will always come first, and "they'll come again".

Another time I was on patrol in one of Nottingham's inner-city suburbs when I heard on the radio that a pursuit had begun nearby. I parked the police car out of sight, grabbed the Stinger from the boot and found a fixed public bin to hide behind. Fortune was on my side this day, and the 'bandit car' headed straight towards me. I was able to stand up from my hiding place at the last minute and throw the Stinger out. It was a good deployment and I managed to get both passenger side tyres, pulling the Stinger back in again before the pursuing police cars went over it too. The fleeing vehicle came to a stop only another couple of hundred yards down the road and the occupants were detained. The driver turned out to be disqualified and had risked the lives of members of the public just to avoid a likely fine and further disqualification. As I was later writing my statement for the incident I was contacted by the officer who'd been leading the pursuit. He told me that he had watched the in-car footage back some three or four times and *still* couldn't see where I was hiding; describing me as a ninja!

This is how Stingers should be deployed, and it makes me cringe when I see police reality TV shows where cops are stood in high-vis jackets next to their marked police cars, blue lights still on waiting to Sting a fleeing vehicle. Nine times out of ten the offender sees the really obvious trap and manages to avoid it. Even worse is cops that stand waiting in the middle of the road or without any kind of cover to deploy the Stinger. This is incredibly dangerous as they're highly likely to be run over by the driver desperate to get away. This is tragically how Merseyside PC Dave Phillips was killed in the line of duty in 2015, when he was deliberately driven at by a fleeing driver he was waiting to stop with a Stinger.

In another example of the benefits of the ANPR system, a car flagged up as having been involved in a bilking – making off without paying for petrol – earlier that day. Sure enough my luck was in again (*or do you make your own luck?*) and I found it nearby moments later. I pulled in behind it and signalled for it to stop, but it continued to drive without pulling over, albeit at normal road speeds. This continued for a couple of streets before he must have plucked up the courage to go for it, accelerating hard and heading straight into the city centre. His manner of driving through the busy city in the middle of the afternoon meant that I had to abort the pursuit barely after it had begun. But in a situation that developed like something off *The Bill* though, the police helicopter had just finished at another job nearby, so was already in the air and only about 30 seconds away. A dog officer had been at the same incident and travelled over as well. Nottingham city centre is one of the areas most densely covered by CCTV in the country. The camera operators were soon able to pick up the car and provide a commentary over the police radio about where it was going. This allowed the helicopter to get above it and direct the dog man to the cul-de-sac where the driver casually got out, thinking he had made good his escape. The dog officer and I were on him in seconds, taking him completely by surprise.

The car turned out to have been stolen the previous week and was on false number plates. The driver wasn't charged with the theft of the car though as he claimed to have just bought it, and we couldn't prove it was him that took it. He was charged with the petrol theft and driving offences and went straight to the top of the list of the unluckiest criminals I've ever dealt with, having been caught in the manner he was. It was like an episode of *The Bill*, where all the right resources needed were available instantly and at the right location to help bring the suspect to justice. This was particularly memorable as nothing like it had happened to me before or since throughout my career!

***

It is sadly a rare thing indeed as an officer to witness criminals getting what you would feel is real justice. Often the sentences handed out by courts are disappointing; especially when you've put a lot of time and effort into building a good case. This isn't necessarily always the courts' fault as they are bound by national sentencing guidelines. An excellent piece of legislation does exist though, to help ensure crime doesn't pay and can be used to hit those who profit from illegal activities twice. The Proceeds of Crime Act (POCA) allows the police and courts to assess the earnings made by criminals as a result of their illegal enterprises and then issue confiscation orders for that amount. If the convicted criminals fail to pay then they can be given several additional years imprisonment and *still* owe the money when they come out. These orders follow them for life meaning that if they get legitimate jobs in future or buy cars or property that can be linked to them, it can be forfeited.

Perhaps my favourite demonstration of the power of this law followed a time when the officers in the unmarked car had noticed a male acting suspiciously. Another chap had appeared out of a nearby house, met up with the first one and handed over several large laundry bags, which the original male put into the boot of his car. A check of the car revealed it had intelligence linking it and the occupant to drug supply. Shortly after it pulled away from the house and once we were sure it was out of sight, we stopped and searched both the occupant and the car. Sure enough the large laundry bags were full to the brim with bulk bags of cannabis. The driver was arrested and sat in the police car, which we drove back to near the original house. A colleague stayed with him whilst the rest of us went to the address to try to arrest the occupant – who we now wanted on suspicion of supplying cannabis.

If someone is wanted in connection with a serious offence and the police believe them to be in an address, officers have a power to enter without a warrant – contrary to the belief of many people who start shouting "you can't come in without a warrant" at officers trying to make such arrests. A quick knock on the door by the plain clothes officers to try and get the male to answer the door didn't work, so then those of us in uniform started to try and force entry. Unfortunately the door was a new composite door which are notoriously difficult to break down – the enforcer just bounces off them.

Whilst we were trying to batter the door down, we could hear through the open upstairs bathroom window that the toilet was being flushed repeatedly. This is bad news for police trying to catch someone with a lot of drugs in their house, as the repeated toilet flushing invariably means that the person inside is trying to flush their stash. Better to get rid of the drugs and owe someone the money for them when you're able to pay it back by selling more, rather than have the drugs seized by the police, go to prison, and then still owe the debt when you come out.

Whilst my colleagues were frantically trying to kick the front door in and get other officers travelling with circular saw to cut the door open, I was trying to smash the soil pipe with my ASP hoping that whatever was being flushed away would spill over the patio instead of down the drain. This way we could recover whatever was being disposed of. Sadly the soil pipe was made of very thick plastic and despite my best efforts I wasn't able to smash it. A few minutes later the other officers arrived with the circular saw and managed to saw the door off and gain entry. We ran in and in the upstairs bathroom we found the male we had first seen handing the bag over, frantically dumping handfuls of cannabis into the toilet. The floor of the bathroom was barely visible for all the cannabis strewn across it where it had been grabbed out the holdalls it was being stored in and dropped into the loo. There were still dozens of holdalls full of cannabis in the address though – more than enough to demonstrate further intent to supply, as well as the actual supply offence we'd seen to begin with.

The house occupant was arrested, his phones and the drugs seized and bank details obtained for the force's financial investigators to look into his monetary affairs. Evidence on his phone showed that he was quite a high-level supplier and some of the messages contained quite serious threats sent to his runners, about using violence to enforce debts that they owed to him. The real satisfaction came from the financial investigator's work however, as they discovered that he owned a whole second property, almost completely mortgage free. Statements the investigators obtained from the bank showed that the arrested man had been paying the mortgage off in cash every month. There were no records of him receiving income from any kind of paid employment. How he was able to pay his mortgage off in cash over the bank counter every month without raising any alarm bells is beyond me.

As a result of this brilliant investigation by the financial investigator, the court ordered the chap to pay back the value of this second house – well over £100,000 worth, as proceeds of crime. We had literally cost this male his home, but there couldn't be any sympathy as he'd bought it through the proceeds of criminal activity. I was told only a few months later by the financial investigators that the man had sold the house whilst he was in prison and the order had been paid. When the police seize assets like this, the force leading the investigation gets to keep a third, and the remainder goes to the treasury; unless a specific victim can be identified who it can be returned to. This provides the seizing forces a real incentive to conduct these investigations, and the financial investigators pay for themselves many times over. The seized money is often used to fund additional services like diversionary activities for young people on the fringes of falling into a life of crime, or for supporting abuse victims who have left everything behind to start a new life away from their abusers. It's a perfect use of this money that was acquired by illegal means, often off the back of the suffering of others.

***

That wasn't the only occasion where the Proceeds of Crime Act came into play, although it was probably my favourite example. The offence of money laundering, or possession of criminal property as it is more formally known, allows law enforcement agencies to seize assets and prosecute people if those items can be identified as the benefit of criminal activities. It also allows police to go after people who are living well beyond their apparent means. Nowhere was this more obvious than the time we stopped a very naïve drug dealer.

This drug dealer didn't fit the stereotype for someone of his profession, which goes to show that stereotypes aren't always helpful. He was from a fairly middle-class background, had a respectable full-time job and no prior criminal record. He was seen by the team appearing to make a deal from his car to a pedestrian in Radford, one of Nottingham's inner-city suburbs. He was surprisingly obvious about what he was doing, driving around in a top of the range high-spec Mercedes, in a suburb where the local postcode gang had a pretty established monopoly on the drugs supply. He was clearly not part of this gang. Not only did this make him easy for us to see, but would have made him a very likely target for some serious violence as a warning to him if the local gang had come across him first.

He was signalled to pull over and initially failed to do so. Clearly not having any criminal past or presumably any criminal connections from whom he had been able to learn the ways of evading the police, he wasn't very successful at it and was stopped a short time later. He and the car were searched and inside we found a reasonable quantity of what later transpired to be ketamine – a class B drug that is legally used as a horse tranquiliser but popular on the party scene.

Once in custody we went and searched his house, which turned out to be his family home where he had a bedroom – but we were told by his family, as is so often the case, that he doesn't actually live there. In his favour as a criminal, was the fact that at least he wasn't naïve enough to have provided us his correct address; which he had apparently kept secret from his family as well. Unfortunately for him, for reasons only known to himself, he had insured his very expensive Mercedes to a different address. A quick trip there and a test of the door key that was on the car key fob and the door magically opened. A second premises search authority was granted for that address by the Inspector and incredibly several kilograms worth of ketamine was found just laying around the flat!

As part of the subsequent investigation his financials were looked into and it was established that his car was on a PCP hire plan costing him some £600 a month and the flat where the drugs were found was rented at £1400 a month. His job barely paid more than minimum wage though, earning him about £19,000 a year, which translates as about £1300 a month before tax. I'm no mathematician, but those sums don't add up... The car was instantly returned to the dealership and POCA orders were made for several thousand pounds on top of his conviction for drug supply. As to why he was drawn into selling drugs in the first place, that has remained a mystery. Presumably the lavish lifestyle that he'd led for several months had suggested to him that it was easy money and something that he could get away with. Maybe the minimum wage entry-level job was not the lifestyle to which he was previously accustomed and he needed to supplement it somehow. It did go to demonstrate that all the criminological theories in the world about why people can become involved in serious crime, cannot account for the pure and simple fact in some people of human greed.

***

It wasn't all just weapons and drugs that we dealt with on the Knife Crime Team. Being a pro-active team means that you can come across all manner of other activities when you check vehicles and people who catch your eye. We made several arrests of alleged rapists, suspected human traffickers, people wanted for failing to attend court or fugitives wanted by other countries amongst other things. We also came across a whole variety of offences that having the advantage of being in unmarked cars can allow you to see – if you know where to look and have a pro-active mindset.

One of these completely different offences that we uncovered turned out to be an elaborate large-scale 'crash for cash' scam. These are where vehicle collisions were staged or didn't even happen and claims for whiplash (or "whip*cash*") were made to insurance companies. We stumbled across this particular instance following a routine stop of a suspicious vehicle. The driver pulled up outside his home address and as colleagues from the team approached him, he ran into the house and closed the door. Very unluckily for him a small quantity of drugs were visible in the car – only consistent with personal use – but this gave us a power of entry into the address to go and arrest him for that offence.

After entering the house and finding the male, we arrested him on suspicion of the possession of drugs (a power of entry only exists without a warrant to effect an arrest of the wanted person). Because we'd now arrested him in the address though, we had a further power to search for other items linked to the offence. As we were now in there anyway, there was no harm in searching it for further drugs – especially as he had run off from us. Hidden in wardrobes in the bedroom though was something that we hadn't expected to find in our wildest imaginations. There were bundles and bundles of £20 and £50 notes – wrapped up how they're portrayed in films, in elastic bands of £1000. After a quick check of one of these bundles confirmed that there was £1000 in it, we counted a staggering 43 bundles, equating to a likely £43,000. We realised that we had stumbled into something much bigger than we'd first anticipated, so we were joined by the rest of the team to help secure the occupants and search the rest of the house. In the same bedroom were plastic crates full of paperwork relating to different vehicles, and letters from insurance firms and claims management companies going back years, all addressed to different people.

This was well outside our sphere of knowledge so we hastily got on the phone to the Fraud Team who came out and joined us to review everything we'd discovered. All the cash and documents were seized and the occupants of the address – about six of them – were all arrested and interviewed by the Fraud Team. Taking all the boxes out the house to the police cars felt like a scene from TV or the news where officers are seen carrying boxes after boxes out of houses that have been raided. I'm not sure what happened to the people arrested that day as the Fraud Team took on the investigation, but I can be fairly confident that the money will not have been returned to them - yet more money recovered from criminal enterprise that has been returned to benefit the local community.

As it happened on that day, we had a special constable out on attachment with us. After we'd found so many exhibits in the house I took her back to the police station to fetch an additional car to help put everything that we'd seized in. As we got back to the address, she dropped the keys to the car down a really inconveniently located grate in the road. Even worse was that it was a plain car that we'd hired, and there wasn't a spare key for it, so it had to be recovered by the police recovery garage! The quality and quantity of cakes due for a cake fine is dependent on the severity of the offence. We had some particularly expensive and tasty cakes that day.

The Fraud Team took another investigation off us a few weeks later, again following an ANPR hit. The vehicle in question had a marker suggesting that the previous day it had been involved in paying for expensive goods with what had turned out to be counterfeit currency. The car was registered and insured to a male who was already on our radar from previous stops and being connected to weapons. We located the vehicle and no sooner than we had got behind it than it pulled over of its own accord. The passenger hastily got out and walked straight into the nearest business – a kids' soft play centre of all things. I was the passenger of our car so I got out and went to detain him and my partner carried on after the car, stopping it around the corner.

Speaking to the passenger, he had no children and it was blatantly apparent that he'd only got out to see if the police were following him, although he of course denied this. He presumably thought it would force us to make a choice whether we stuck with him or went after the car. Unfortunately for him there were two of us and we could get both of them. We also had back-up nearby who came to join us so that we had the numbers to control the subjects and search the car. Sure enough, both passenger and driver had significant quantities of £20 notes on them, all mysteriously bearing the same serial number and no watermarks... Two arrests later and the Fraud Team once again took the job from us. It turned out that the pair had been using the counterfeit currency in dozens of shops all across the city. There had been dozens of incidents called in to the police the previous day about them, all describing the same pair. Many of the shops they'd targeted had good CCTV and the shop keepers were also able to provide descriptions of them both, who were quite distinctive in their appearance. Both got charged with about a dozen offences each, as well as the possession of counterfeit currency that we found on them. They were later convicted on all counts after pleading guilty and received some reasonable custodial sentences.

***

One of our best drugs supply jobs came in the early days of the team, and also help to prove the value of some of our alternative disruption tactics. My colleagues had stopped a car and were speaking to the driver who had recent intelligence about drugs supply. A search found that he had a small amount of cannabis on him, but also several phones. This wasn't enough to arrest him on suspicion of intent to supply, but he did admit to being a regular cannabis user – presumably intending to make us believe the cannabis in the car was his for personal use.

Around this time new legislation had come into force allowing the police to test drivers for drugs at the roadside. A new offence had also been created of driving over the specified limit of various drugs, which hadn't existed before. Being passionate about roads policing matters, I'd been trained in their use at a very early stage following the force getting the new kits, and had taken these with me to the Knife Crime Team. I realised that if we could get suspected drug dealers driving bans, they wouldn't be able to go and deliver their drugs to their customers and would have to rely on others, possibly more naïve, to drive them around. It would also frustrate their abilities to go and 'reload' their own supply stash and deny them hiding places in cars to avoid detection if stopped by police. I'd shown the value of this power to the team only recently before this stop, when I'd secured a three-year driving ban for a high level Organised Crime Group member, and was awaiting a court date for another one.

We swabbed the driver who tested positive for cannabis. This meant we had to arrest him and take him to custody to obtain an evidential blood sample and could deal with him for the cannabis possession offence at the same time. My partner and I took him to the station whilst my other colleagues continued on patrol. About ten minutes later they shouted up over the radio for one of us to go and join them ASAP. I was the driver so I jumped in the police car leaving my partner to continue dealing with the prisoner. I arrived to find they'd detained two males who'd run from a car. The cops had been watching them from the plain car and seen what they thought was some kind of exchange between the car occupants, one of whom had just got in after walking there from a nearby address. As they'd got out the plain car and walked over to speak to the suspicious pair, the passenger got out. On seeing two people walking towards them with purpose he ran off. The officers had given chase and shouted "police officers" whilst putting on their police baseball caps that we used to identify ourselves with. On seeing this the running man threw a cricket ball-seized item over the roof of the nearby houses before he was caught and detained by my fleet-footed colleague.

The other officer had detained the car's driver and they'd asked me to join them so I could look after the two detainees in the marked car whilst they searched for whatever had been thrown by the runner. When they found it, they discovered a cling film ball containing a massive lump of cocaine. Some further officers from the local neighbourhood team came to join us and one of them watched the two detainees whilst we gained entry to the passenger's address.

Before we even got into the address we could smell the overwhelming stench of cannabis coming from inside and weren't disappointed with what we found. Bag after one-ounce bag of cannabis was clearly in the process of being bagged up into smaller individual street deal bags. I think we recovered between 12 – 14Oz of cannabis from the address as well as more class A drugs and evidence to show that the drugs were being prepared for sale. This was clearly the stash flat that the drugs were being prepared and stored in for onward sale. Most surprisingly, and in one of the most serendipitous finds of my career, I located the driving licence of the chap we already had in custody for the drug driving matter! There were also several letters addressed to him at this address and paperwork in his name. We hastily contacted our colleague at the custody suite and told him not to release the suspect, and instead to arrest him on suspicion of drug supply offences!

We lodged both our new arrestees at the custody suite and seized their phones. Crucially on the search we found bulk loads of drug dealer business cards. These have a phone number on and are given out to customers who can make their drugs orders by phone and have them delivered to them by the dealer, just like ordering takeaway food. "Food" is even a street slang term for drugs, probably for this reason. (This is essentially how County Lines drug dealing works, but was commonly used in the cities long before being exported to rural towns and villages.) We took all the seized items back to the station, where one of the phones used by the original car driver we'd arrested earlier was ringing off-the-hook and text messages were coming through thick and fast. Luckily for us the content of these messages appeared on the phone lock screen which were clearly asking for drugs deliveries. This made us think that this phone was in fact the 'line phone' – the handset with the SIM card in that matched the number on the business cards. We rang the phone number on the business cards from one of our office phones and sure enough the driver's phone rang. Just to be sure we did the same again and the phone rang again. Getting the 'line phone' is like hitting the goldmine, as they're always full of messages related to drugs supply. It also takes the phone out of service for a while and renders all the existing business cards that have been handed out obsolete, forcing the dealers to almost start from scratch again. Good fortune and the disruption tactic of DrugWiping (drug saliva testing) the driver had ensured that we already had him in custody and meant that he couldn't dispose of his phones. Very, very occasionally, luck deals you a perfect hand and this was one of those occasions. Both the original driver and the passenger whose address we found the drugs in were convicted of possession with intent to supply class A and B drugs and received hefty prison sentences, especially the original car driver who couldn't deny he played a leading role in the organisation, as he was in possession of the main drugs line phone.

The DrugWipe proved itself again following the stop of a car that was linked by intelligence to drugs supply. A search at the roadside was negative, but once again the driver failed the screening drugs test. Getting someone linked to drugs supply off the road was a small win in itself anyway as a consolation prize. I took him to custody, where we went through all the procedure of obtaining a blood sample to send off for analysis, getting his fingerprints and photographs and bailing the chap pending the forensics results. I thought no more of it until I came in the following day to an e-mail from one of the custody staff saying that they had recovered a small bag of white powder from the floor of the cell block that they believed was cocaine. The CCTV footage showed it dropping out the shorts of my prisoner as we'd been leaving the previous day! As previously mentioned, we couldn't and didn't strip search everyone detained and there just hadn't been grounds to strip search this particular man. He'd *so nearly* managed to get away with whatever he was secreting in his underwear, but his luck had run out just as he was about to get away with it.

As a team we went round to his house straight away and after initially surrounding the house to ensure he didn't run out the back when we knocked on the door (a common escape used by the baddies and always embarrassing for officers when it happens). He answered the door and I arrested him on the doorstep for possession of cocaine. This meant that I had a power to enter and search the address for further drugs – people don't tend to secrete personal use amounts in their underwear. Because we had our suspect detained, my colleagues from the garden came round to the front and we all went in to begin the search. The first question we'd always ask was "are we going to find anything?" to which the chap answered "I don't have anything, but my two friends are upstairs and they might have brought stuff with them, I don't know." This took us by surprise as we weren't expecting anyone else at the address, certainly not the pair he named, so my colleagues quickly ran upstairs, only to find a wide-open rear window and a pair of footprint tracks in the dewy grass of the rear garden below. It appeared that after my colleagues had come back round to the front the other pair had seen that the coast was clear and gone out the window at the back! They'd handily left behind their phones and even a driving licence in their haste, but clearly there was something in the house that they didn't want to be caught with, unless they'd taken that with them too.

Sure enough a search of the address uncovered a Tupperware container hidden in a cupboard in the room where the pair had escaped from, full of multiple types of class A and B drugs, cash and scales. The biggest and best find however was a laundry bag full of what looked like herbs. It had no smell so wasn't cannabis, but we seized it and after being sent to forensics was found to be mamba (spice); nearly 1kg of the stuff. The value of the drugs recovered ran into the tens of thousands of pounds. We also recovered business cards, lighters and cannabis grinders which all had a phone number stuck on them, like some kind of drug dealer loyalty rewards!

One of the phones we seized had that number's SIM card in, and was full of messages linking it to one of the two men named as having been in the house that fled out the window. This was one of the most complex investigations that I ever conducted, as I had to link the pair who fled the scene to the drugs without us having physically caught them there. Luckily some excellent help from numerous other departments within the police, overt and covert, meant that I could definitively link the main male we were after to the drugs. The chap whose house it was that we arrested at the doorstep pleaded guilty to allowing his premises to be used for the preparation of drugs and was given a suspended sentence.

Sadly the case occurred at a time there was a significant delay in processing forensic evidence due to a significant legal issue around one of the country's main forensic laboratories. Its complexities added further delays, meaning it was some two years before it was listed for trial. The man I'd linked to the phone contested the charge so the case was sent for a full trial, a normal delay of between six to nine further months. Victimless cases – where there are no direct victims or witnesses other than police officers – are always (rightly) given a lower priority at court so if there are insufficient jurors or courts available etc then they are postponed to a future date. That happened to this case and the additional delays pushed it into the summer of 2020. By this time the pandemic had struck and all courts except remand cases were put on hold, further adding to the delay. The demands on courts as a result of this situation was such that there was incredible pressure on the Crown Prosecution Service (CPS) and the police to avoid prosecuting anything that they could.

Due to the complexities of this case the trial would have lasted for a week or so, taking up a significant amount of very scarce court time. When the suspect I'd spent so long building the case up against offered to plead guilty to possession with intent to supply the mamba (which had his fingerprint on the bag) the CPS jumped at the chance to remove this complex trial from the backlog and accepted the plea, dropping the rest of the charges. The chap who I'd spent some two years building a comprehensive case against for being a higher-level class A drug dealer, was able to 'escape' with a relatively minor conviction. He was only given a community rehabilitation order with unpaid work and a fine, with a short suspended sentence to hang over him for a couple of years. I only found out this result after leaving the police, and it was gutting after I had put so much time and effort into the investigation. This is typical of the situation resulting from the pandemic, where as many cases as possible were being dropped to reduce the backlog at court. My own experience with this and countless other cases, as well as anecdotal accounts from colleagues all supports this.

***

Another unlucky person that we dealt with on the Knife Crime Team happened to attract the eye of one of the team members by driving like a bit of plank through some quiet residential streets. If there's one thing guaranteed to get the attention of a passing police car then it's substandard driving. A prompt turn-in-the-road and they went after him, only to see that he had seen the police car spinning round to go after him, abandoned the car and was now running down the road on foot. My colleagues were out and after him like a flash, chasing him down alleyways between houses and detaining him in gardens after surrounding the area and use of good searching skills. They arrested him and took him to custody where he didn't want to provide us with his address. Unfortunately for him we were searching his car and found several pieces of paperwork in it linking him to an address only a few doors up from where the car was. A quick authorisation from the Inspector and we went and searched that address. The entire loft conversion room was filled to the brim with cannabis smoking paraphernalia. On examining the items it became apparent that this chap had his own semi-legitimate business operating a stall at festivals selling cannabis smoking paraphernalia such as large cigarette rolling papers; plastic cannabis joint holders to stop them getting crushed; bongs; grinders etc. This was reminiscent of the head shops I had raided during my time as a beat manager, except this male took his wares on the road. As with the fixed shops his trade was dubious legally, but he was presumably using the same get-out clause the shop owners were in that people can do what they want with the innocent items that he sold and it's not his fault.

The unfortunate thing for him however was the dozen or more large protein powder buckets in the same room that all had remnants of cannabis in them. There was also bin liner upon bin liner of very dry, very old stalks of cannabis plants. Clearly this chap knew exactly what he was doing with the paraphernalia he was selling. Even so, a prosecution for supplying drugs paraphernalia of this kind would be difficult. What was less difficult for us to prove was the large compressed block of reddy-brown coloured powder that we found hidden under the bed and the press next to it. This was a device that would normally be for compressing wood or paper pulp into bricks for an open fire, except this one had residue of the same reddy-brown powder inside it.

As a result of the large quantity of the remnants of cannabis and what we suspected to be heroin we seized everything, including all the drugs smoking paraphernalia. After forensic tests the reddy-brown substance did transpire to be heroin. The male got a brace of years in prison for possession with intent to supply class A drugs. All because he couldn't drive properly and didn't want to face into that with the police. Had he pulled over and spoken to cops he probably would have just got a warning about his driving standards.

It's incredible how often people up to no good give themselves away when they see a police car. Lingering at a give way junction just a little too long to allow a police car to pass; intentionally not looking at a police officer, or staring them out; suddenly walking off after having been loitering in one spot. All are tell-tale subconscious behaviours people exhibit when faced with a possible consequence to their actions. And luckily all are easy to spot for an experienced pro-active officer.

There is a well-known psychological theory about the fear of being watched, that is especially relevant to crime-fighting. A famous experiment at Newcastle University showed that simply by putting pictures of a pair of eyes near to frequently attacked bicycle rack reduced thefts of bikes from it by some 63%.[*] This same tactic is used at locations across the country for different things: shops that regularly experience shoplifting put a cardboard police officer in the window and thefts go down; petrol stations put signs up

---

[*] Nettle D, Nott K, Bateson M (2012) 'Cycle Thieves, We Are Watching You': Impact of a Simple Signage Intervention against Bicycle Theft. *PLoS ONE* 7(12):e51738.

warning of CCTV and ANPR and drive-offs go down; police put signs out saying "operation in progress" in burglary hotspot areas and burglaries go down. It's something to do with the evolved instinct humans have to be afraid of consequences and to have a subconscious reaction in case a potential predator or rival tribe was watching you. Science and psychology is fascinating, and the new police training methods involving university inputs allows new officers to gain an understanding of these kind of theories, and I enjoy teaching them. Hopefully it will lead to even more new and innovative ways to reduce crime in the future as these officers progress up the ranks.

***

Sometimes luck was on our side and other times we made our own luck. I've already shown that criminals like to try and hide items so that they don't get found by the police, and on someone's body there's only limited opportunities for that. In a car however there are a hundred and one places that drugs can be hidden. For reasons of not wanting to give away secrets that could be used against the police I won't divulge these locations, but there are loads of common ones that any good pro-active team soon gets to know. The benefits of experience in knowing these locations came to the fore on a couple of memorable occasions during my stint on the Knife Crime Team. I learned about them from watching the more experienced team members conducting searches and was then able to pass this knowledge on to the newer team members and officers on attachment who came to work with us later on.

One such occasion I was out on patrol in the plain car and turned onto a street where I was literally blocked by a car stopped in the middle of the road right in front of me. I saw someone come out the adjacent house, walk up the window of the car, pass cash in, get given something small in his hand and the car drive off again. There was little doubt that I had just witnessed a drug deal take place right in front of me. I radioed for my colleagues to come to me, giving a commentary whilst I followed the suspect, waiting for the marked car to come and get it stopped. We were keen not to show out the plain car whenever possible (criminals would take pictures and share them round social media), so I drove past where they stopped the suspect, parked round the corner, got out and walked casually to join my colleagues. I made sure to put on my baseball cap when the guy we'd stopped wasn't looking, to make it look like I had been in the police car all along.

I was absolutely positive that there were drugs in that car or on the driver – I'd just seen the deal happen – and unless he'd just sold his last deal, they'd be in there somewhere. My colleagues were already searching the car, and when they finished told me there was nothing in it. This didn't add up, so I went over and did my own search, checking some of the less obvious hiding places that I'd previously come across. As soon as I removed some of the car interior panelling I hit the jackpot, and stuffed in there was a freezer bag containing all manner of different coloured powders and tablets. I called my colleague over to show him the hiding place and what I'd found. I then went and broke the good news to the driver and put the handcuffs on him. My colleague was kicking himself for missing it, but he'd only recently joined the team and every officer has learning experiences like this, it's how everyone learns. He was certainly sure to never miss anything again, and we all invested in multi-tools which were great for prizing plastic cowling off and led us to find loads of secret stashes. The colleague who'd missed the find went to the suspect's address for the search and found several thousands of pounds in cash that was very well-hidden and could have easily been missed on a less thorough search, completely vindicating him. This money was later forfeited under the Proceeds Oof Crime Act and the male was sentenced to three years in custody.

We also had attachment officers joining us from emergency response teams for month-long periods to learn these very skills and improve their pro-active abilities. I was taking one of these officers out with me one evening when we spotted a dodgy looking car which we decided to stop and check. Intelligence checks and a smell of cannabis gave us enough to search the clearly very nervous driver and the car. I waited with the driver sat in the back of our police car whilst my colleague went to search his car. He came back to tell me that the boot was full of boxes of the previously described dealer business cards, and there was a set of scales in the glove box. He also highlighted to me that there was a screwdriver in the driver's door pocket and no other tools, so it was possibly there as a weapon. Other than that he couldn't find anything illegal.

I was intrigued to see the business cards and the screwdriver that my colleague had specifically mentioned, so went to have a look for myself. There were two full boxes of business cards, clearly just come from the printers and the scales had residue of drugs on, but of itself this is not really enough evidence to arrest someone on. It's certainly not enough to get a conviction from, so not worth wasting time on a 'fishing trip' on the off-chance he had drugs at his home address or similar. Seeing these dealing paraphernalia and how nervous the detained chap still was, I was once again sure that there were drugs somewhere in the car. This was again the 'Copper's Nose' instinct that develops in officers as they lengthen their service and develop their skills based on their experiences. Suddenly it hit me. *The screwdriver.* It was only a small electricity detecting screwdriver and there were no other tools in the car. It certainly wasn't any use as a weapon due to being so small, so why was it on its own in the driver's door pocket?

I began to check around the driver's cockpit area and saw that on one of the interior surfaces there were scratch marks next to a join between two bits of the plastic cowling. The flat head of the screwdriver slid perfectly under the join in the trim and off popped the plastic. Sure enough, there was the clear plastic freezer bag hidden in the void. Pulling it out I could see that inside were numerous different varieties of so-called party drugs – MDMA, cocaine, ketamine and cannabis. I stood back up out the car and held the bag up for my colleague to see. Sat behind him the detained driver in the back of the police car visibly slumped and put his head in his hands. He must have been beginning to think he'd got away with it and now the reality hit harder than a smack in the face. I walked back over to the police car and unsurprisingly my colleague was disappointed at missing the find when I explained where it had been. He was kicking himself, but I reassured him that everyone misses things and it was experiences like this why the attachment system was in place. He could take these searching skills back to his shift and share the knowledge wider. The male was arrested and his phone seized, on which we found loads of messages relating to drugs supply. As we couldn't test the drugs immediately, we had to bail him.

He subsequently failed to appear in court and was arrested months later by another force after a high-speed pursuit up a motorway after which he'd abandoned the car and ran off across fields, attempting to throw another full bag of drugs away. Sadly for him by that point the police helicopter was overhead and caught the whole thing on film. He was sentenced at the same court hearing for both offences; the fact that he'd carried on dealing drugs whilst on bail and on the run after failing to appear at court did him no favours at all. Liberty was a thing he would not get to experience for some seven years.

***

I too made mistakes during my time on the team. Perhaps the most notable was a time when I saw a male I'd recently arrested for knife possession sat in the driver's seat of a parked car. The car hadn't been there when I passed ten minutes earlier and I knew that he was a disqualified driver, but hadn't seen him driving it so couldn't prove that he had. I still stopped and spoke to him to remind him that we were around and knew who he was. Routine checks of the car showed that it didn't have any insurance or tax. The police can seize vehicles that have no tax parked on public roads on behalf of the DVLA, and given that this male was linked to knife crime and had connections to a local gang I informed him that I would be taking the car. Mysteriously he claimed to not have the key and we had no power to search him for it. It didn't matter though as the recovery company could just drag the car up onto their flatbed truck.

Whilst waiting for the recovery truck to arrive the chap kept going into and coming out of a nearby building and was then joined by several other men who were all linked to the same gang. It always gave me great pleasure in knowing people's names as it makes them often think twice about trying anything when they realise that you know who they are so they're less likely to get away with whatever they might consider doing. I greeted all of the group personally and got the usual chelp back from them about not having better things to be doing and 'police harassment', but it was water off a duck's back to me when we experienced this kind of chat on a daily basis, interacting with the type of people that we did. Bizarrely though whilst talking to them the car kept getting locked and unlocked as the indicators were flashing and then one of them would get something out, but of course no-one was forthcoming with the keys still...

The recovery truck arrived and as it began loading the car, a man came out of a house further up the road who started shouting and swearing loudly at my colleague and me. This took our attention off the car and the group of males we'd been speaking to because we were trying to get this strangely abusive chap to calm down and go back into his address. Suddenly behind me I heard an engine start up so I turned around to see the original chap I'd stopped sat in the driver's seat of the car that we were trying to recover. I ran over to him just as he pulled out from the side of the road, and managed to draw my ASP baton. I successfully smashed the driver's window as he drove almost at me, which forced me to jump out the way.

My colleague ran back to our police car to try and catch up with the male, and even the recovery driver jumped back into his truck and shouted to me to get in and we had a look around the area for it too, joined by several other police units. After five minutes or so we found the car parked unattended on a nearby side street and had it recovered from there. I found the male the following day at his home address, arrested and interviewed him and he was charged with several offences. He received a six-month custodial sentence at court.

Looking back, it's clear to me that there must have been something that the group seriously did not want the police to find in the car. Why else would the chap who was fully aware that I knew his name and that he wouldn't be able to get away with his actions, do what he did? If he'd just let us take it at the roadside for no tax, he wouldn't have even faced any action because we couldn't show he had driven it or that the car was his. He knew by driving off in it though that he would be facing several charges as a result and prison time would have been a real consideration. He took the car anyway, only to leave it abandoned a few streets away where we would be sure to find it later. My only conclusion is that there must have either been a gun or a large quantity of drugs in the car for him to do what he did, which he was able to take out and secrete elsewhere in the five minutes time he bought himself. Sadly I'll never know and it was a significant missed opportunity to remove whatever contraband it was from the streets. Whether the group had somehow contacted the angry man to come and provide a distraction, or it was just very fortunate timing allowing them the two minutes needed to get in the car and drive off I don't know.

***

During my three years on the Knife Crime Team I was involved in the seizure or recovery of some near 300 weapons, including the aforementioned firearms, knives, axes and extendable batons. On top of this was hundreds of thousands of pounds in suspected criminal cash and hundreds of kilograms of drugs. This kind of work is exactly why I got into policing and made a definitive positive impact on the communities we served. It is hard to think of many other police teams, especially with only six members, who made such an impact on Nottingham, measured by the massive amount of jail time issued to people we arrested and the drugs, weapons and cash removed from the streets. The potential harm in the form of stabbings, additional drug addicts, exploitation of young people and criminal lifestyles we prevented by removing these things from the streets cannot be measured. This gives me an enormous sense of pride, and I know that the team continue to achieve great results still with limited numbers. They have recently featured heavily on the popular TV show *Police Interceptors* as a result of their outstanding successes.

It was so nearly not to be however. The team was established in early 2016, right at the height of Home Secretary Theresa May's 'war on stop and search' which saw the number of searches performed by the police plummet from 1.3 million a year nationally in 2009 to a low of just over 240,000 in April 2018.[*]. Meanwhile at the same time, knife crimes nearly doubled from around 24,000 in the 2013-14 financial year, to over 46,000 in 2019-20.[†] This is no academic study into whether these are correlated, but I don't think it needs much more than common sense to suggest that there is some kind of link. Setting up a pro-active team dedicated to stopping and searching people was a very bold move by the senior officers at the time and is a credit to them. I suspect it was more around the politics of being seen to try and arrest the trend of rising knife crime, but whatever the motives it has proven a huge success. The communities the team have been to have all been really supportive of our actions, as they understand stop and search, whilst controversial, is necessary. We did it in a targeted, intelligence led manner, treating those we stopped with respect

---

[*] Office of National Statistics data
[†] UK Parliament data

wherever possible – sometimes as I've said it's necessary to go in at a higher level to prevent injury.

There were a couple of occasions we'd stop people who we had credible intel that they were actively carrying a knife, and pinned them straight up against a wall or trapped their arms. It's just not worth taking the risk of standing near them and asking politely "excuse me sir, are you carrying a hunting knife by any chance?" You can bet they'd either draw it on you or run off. These tactics were always explained to both them after they were secured though, and the community scrutiny panels, who independently review stop and searches, later.

There was also another reason that participating in the team very nearly didn't happen for me personally though, when soon after joining it, one of my closest friends in the force and one of the most pro-active no-nonsense officers I ever met, was investigated as a result of a car stop he conducted. The driver of the car complained to the Professional Standards Department (PSD), alleging that my friend had stopped him solely based on his ethnicity and that excessive force had been used to detain him. I took on the role of his welfare officer to support my friend emotionally through the proceedings – an officially recognised role within the complaints process, but one which it transpired would only be paid lip service by the PSD. I supported my friend throughout the proceedings and attended every day of his four-day gross misconduct hearing, so heard all the facts of the case.

He had been working a night shift when he'd seen a car repeatedly changing lanes on the city's ring road and suspecting the driver may have been drunk or tired, signalled for it to stop. The driver had stopped suddenly in the outside lane, rather than usual practice of pulling to the left, which made the officer more suspicious. Immediately on stopping the driver had got out his car and marched straight over to my friend shouting at him loudly and waving his arms around gesticulating, before the officer had even had a chance to do more than get out his car. Just as my colleague started to try and speak to the driver, he turned round and went to get back in his car, starting the engine. Assuming that there was something not right with the situation and the driver was trying to get away, my colleague followed him and tried to get the keys out the ignition – which I've already described as being one of the most dangerous situations an officer can find themselves in. He succeeded in doing so before the man could drive off, but the man then refused to get out the car. My friend stood in the crook of the driver's door as the man was trying to slam it closed, repeatedly pulling it into my colleague, who was asking the man to get out. Instead the driver then resorted to gripping the steering wheel with both hands with all his strength to prevent himself being pulled out. Trying to get someone out the enclosed and confined space of the cockpit of a car is incredibly difficult at the best of times as it relies largely on just the strength of the one officer who is able to get to their side, versus the strength of the driver latched to the steering wheel. My colleague tried pulling him out to no avail and then attempted to use his baton as a lever to twist the man's arm out. This didn't work either as if his arm came free the man instantly snapped it back onto the steering wheel. There was little other choice than to use the baton to strike the man's arm to get him to release them.

After three baton strikes the male let go of the steering wheel and the officer managed to get him out the car and onto the grass central reservation and arrested him for a public order offence based on the man's behaviour. When other officers arrived and the man had calmed down, he explained that his child was ill in the back of the car and he had been trying to take them to the hospital. As soon as he said this an ambulance was called and the child was taken to hospital for treatment and the man's wife collected and taken to the hospital to be with the child.

After the incident the complaint was made that my friend had stopped the man based on the colour of his skin and that excessive force had been used to detain him. I'm not sure about the casual observer, but in my experience if the man had just come over to the officer and said "I'm really sorry, my child is really ill in the back, can we just get to the hospital and I'll do whatever you need there" then most officers would have absolutely agreed to do that. (I've even given a blue light escort to someone I stopped for speeding who it turned out had his wife in the car who was in labour!) At the most the man would have been kept for a couple of minutes whilst a breath test was done and then been on his way. Instead he charged at the officer ranting loudly and gesticulating angrily, before going straight back to his car and trying to drive off.

The PSD investigation took the best part of a year or more, even though they had the man and the child's statement within a week or so. During this time my colleague was removed from front-line duties and treated abysmally by the investigators, being provided little to no updates about the case and with certainly no explanation for the lengthy delays. Ultimately the PSD cleared him of any wrongdoing, finding that he could not have known the man's ethnicity at the time of the stop because he had been driving behind him, and in the dark. They found that the force used was reasonable and proportionate to remove the man from the car who had been obstructive and refusing to get out.

The complainant wasn't satisfied with this outcome and appealed directly to the Independent Office for Police Conduct (IOPC). The IOPC reviewed the PSD's investigation and decreed that in fact there was a case for gross misconduct and my colleague would have to face a hearing. From my experience and that of any other police officer I've spoken to, the IOPC are anything but independent. They seem far more desirous of hanging cops out to dry and appeasing those who make complaints, most likely as some kind of pseudo-proof that they are definitely not linked to the police. How the IOPC investigators could review a case that trained professional detectives had taken over a year to investigate and come up with a completely different outcome is beyond my understanding.

As per the IOPC mandate, my friend was therefore subject to a gross misconduct hearing. These run very much like a court, with a prosecuting and defence barrister, witnesses, and a three-person panel comprised of a senior HR professional, a senior police officer of at least Superintendent rank, and a trained professional independent panel chair. The PSD are there to support the 'prosecution' barrister and the Police Federation to support the defence. I was there as my friend's welfare officer throughout as well. In the run-up to the hearing we found out who the apparently independent'professional panel chair was; a barrister whose website biography of himself describes him as "specialising in defence of homicide, firearms and drugs suspects" who also "has a keen interest in police brutality cases". This keen interest wholly suggested that a role that should be non-biased would in actual fact be anything but. A check by the Police Federation who kept track of the judgements of all the designated panel chairs showed that in fact to that date this independent chair had not led a single gross misconduct hearing that had not resulted in the instant dismissal of the officer on trial!

The writing was on the wall from the outset. As the hearing progressed even the Superintendent on the panel was asking questions of my friend that were not standard operational practice, undermining my friend significantly, such asking him if he was adhering to old policies that were no longer in place. At the conclusion of the trial my good friend and widely esteemed colleague was dismissed without notice – having previously been completely exonerated on the same evidence. The panel concluded that there was no evidence of racial discrimination but that excessive force had been used. There was no determination about what force *should* have been used to remove the belligerent chap from the car, just that the officer's actions in the space of less than a minute in the face of a man trying to drive off were beyond what would constitute reasonable.

There were significant rumblings of discontent across the whole force as a result of the verdict and outcome, with every officer I spoke to condemning the decision with terms 'witch hunt', 'foregone conclusion' and 'kangaroo court' being commonly used. The general sentiment following the case was to stop undertaking pro-active work as well, given that had my colleague not optionally chosen to stop a suspiciously driven vehicle he would not have ended up in any bother. This was particularly tough for me as my whole role revolved around being pro-active. I can certainly say my enthusiasm waned considerably as a result of this for quite some time, possibly for the remainder of my career. I still always wanted to catch baddies, but occasionally there were moments of indecision about whether to stop and engage with someone where the interaction may turn out to be more confrontational than average.

To top the whole incident off, the day following the conclusion of the hearing, I received an e-mail from the Superintendent in charge of PSD at that time summonsing me to his office. I took my Inspector with me, who was a top boss and really supportive. The Superintendent had clearly intended to give some kind of royal dressing down for my support of my friend, but the tone of this was most likely significantly lowered as a result of my Inspector being there. I was told in no uncertain terms that (in spite of the hearing being open for the public to attend!) I was categorically not to talk about the proceedings to any colleagues. For what reason and on what basis I never was sure. I certainly didn't feel it was any kind of lawful order.

I was also accused of attempting to intimidate the panel members by staring at them – these panel members that are all senior people in their fields. I was suffering from an ear infection at the time that reduced my hearing by about half, and explained this to the Superintendent that I needed to look at people speaking to supplement my hearing by watching their mouths and partially lip read. He seemed to accept this, but I still found it bizarre that people so senior could apparently be intimidated by someone who was not a part of the proceedings and had been sat towards the back of the room in the public gallery. I was also accused of not dressing appropriately, despite being told not to attend in uniform and having worn collared t-shirts and smart jumpers, on my days off! Again, when he knew that it had been my days off he seemed to relax a little, but he hadn't taken the time to ask me by e-mail or similar about this before summonsing me. He then concluded by saying that no welfare officer had attended a hearing before and he wasn't sure what benefit I had brought to the proceedings. When I explained that it was in the Police Regulations that I could be there and had actually helped support my friend at numerous points throughout the process he again changed tack and even suggested that I should work with the PSD to compile an official policy around the role of the welfare officer. They never did contact me.

This whole experience that happened to both my colleague and the way I was treated for being a welfare officer left a very bitter taste in my mouth. This was the first time I ever really considered leaving the police; if they could put a good proactive experienced cop through this rigmarole what was the point of going above and beyond rather than just simply doing the bare minimum and taking the pay cheque home each month? Sadly this was all too common in the police, with no incentive to undertake additional work and actually it often landing you in hot water. Consequently there are all too many officers who just coast through their careers, doing the bare minimum required, sometimes even then only after cajoling from the supervisors. Cops who do go above and beyond are the ones who find themselves in hot water.

For two years in a row on the Knife Crime Team I was the officer with the most stop and searches in the entire force. I also had one of the highest positive outcome rates – where the search would result in an arrest or other criminal justice outcome. I was asked to be a stop and search mentor to help other officers improve their searches, based on the way I conducted them and my recording of the grounds (the reason why we were searching people) being exemplary. But I was never thanked or rewarded for that. Instead, for those two years, and one previously when I was a beat manager, the only reason that I became aware of the list existing was because I was pulled in to see my Inspector.

I was asked to account for why my stop and search rates of BAME individuals was disproportionately high. Essentially I was being accused of being discriminatory and a racist. I was beat manager of Radford, one of the most multi-cultural areas in Nottingham, and when on the Knife Crime Team was predominantly tasked to either Radford again, Forest Fields, Sneinton or St Ann's – perhaps the other most diverse areas of the city. I've already shown how supposed disproportionality is taken from the county-wide ethnicity statistics. When looking at the make-ups of those areas though, my search statistics were broadly in line with that population mix. I pointed that out to the Inspectors (who were simply speaking to me because they'd been told to) and they accepted that was probably correct. But no-one higher than me had apparently considered that. Instead it was easier to accuse me of being a racist and have me try and defend myself. Presumably if I couldn't I'd have been hauled up in front of a more senior officer and then no doubt given some kind of additional diversity awareness training. I'd then have stopped searching anyone not White, no matter what the grounds.

One possible solution to this was identified by Lord Scarman in his report on the Brixton Riots of 1981 – to increase the diversity of the police workforce. The intention here, he asserted, was to ensure the police represented the communities they served, and made officers more familiar with diverse cultural views. I passionately believe that a more diverse police service can only be better for all involved, both for the force itself as a workforce from varied backgrounds increases officers knowledge, understanding and offers different viewpoints at problem solving; but also for the communities the police serve, demonstrating absolute equality of opportunity and understanding around cultural sensitivities. I only ever judged a person or situation on its own merits and never based on protected characteristics. I don't accept the mindless accusations of racial discrimination that are thrown at the police by small self-interest groups, and the sometimes mindless ways that some senior officers come up with to combat that perceived problem. I was being made to answer for my actions, when if I simply didn't search anyone, I'd have been fine to just plod along with no issues.

As time passed and with the support of my amazing wife and excellent colleagues, coupled with my deep-rooted desire to just catch baddies, I continued on the Knife Crime Team and kept doing pro-active work. Sheer good fortune (and I am *certain* that a significant proportion of a police officer completing their full service relies solely on luck at not getting a problematic complaint) meant that I never got in trouble for anything. I would have happily stayed with this team for the remainder of my career considering how much I enjoyed the work, but five years after passing my Sergeant's exam I was finally given an opportunity for promotion. With a young family and a career-average pension to consider, as well having held a desire to move up the rank structure for some time, this was an opportunity I wasn't going to turn down.

Supervision

No more 'Pirate Wednesdays'

In March 2019 I was given the opportunity to take over supervision of a response shift at Radford Road Police Station. This was an area that I knew well, as since the closure of Canning Circus Police Station it covered the same areas I had traditionally always worked. I also knew a large part of the team from my time working as a beat manager, where my shift pattern crossed over all the local response teams' patterns. This shift had also helped me at the incident where I had been slammed into the fridge by the drug dealer and I had worked with them on several other larger jobs as well.

I was taking over from their former Sergeant who had been with the team for perhaps the best part of a decade and was notorious for styling himself as a pirate, for reasons known only to him. He was a larger-than-life character both physically (he was about 6'4" with a large forked beard and booming voice) as well as metaphorically – donning pirate hats and speaking like a pirate (in the office) every Wednesday. Every officer at Radford Road knew about 'Pirate Wednesdays', although I never did work out exactly what the point of it was or why it happened. My arrival meant an end to 'Pirate Wednesdays', although I don't think they were missed by many of the team... I was very lucky that I knew several members of the team already and they me, which made settling in a lot easier and also the team's acceptance of me quicker as they knew what kind of officer I was.

I tried to bring my passion for pro-active policing to the team, which was difficult as a supervisor. For large parts of every set of shifts I was stuck at the desk reviewing ongoing caseloads, outstanding live demand of incidents, being contacted for decisions or advice by my team or doing myriad other admin tasks. Being a Sergeant is often described by officers of that rank or above as being the toughest role in the police. You work closely with the team and are part of it, but also need to be removed from it so as to be able to deal with any issues that might arise with any of your subordinates. You also have a modicum of power and authority to be able to order people to do things, but ultimately bigger decisions are made still well above your rank. It's then your job to enforce those decisions and manage any moaning or opposition by the team, whether you agree with the initiative or not.

That aside, I relished this opportunity. The team were great and by-and-large hard working. All were really accepting of me and a lot of the younger officers with short lengths of service especially were really keen and had a real talent. I was eager to provide as many development opportunities as I could for anyone who wanted them and ensured numerous members of my team received both training in different skills and attachments to other departments wherever possible.

As a Sergeant I was required to attend all the more serious incidents and provide on-the-ground leadership and direction. This meant that I became involved in several more interesting goings-on. I was especially keen to demonstrate that I would not ask my team to do anything that I was not prepared to do myself, often taking the lead whenever circumstances allowed. Perhaps the most serious incident that I attended happened one afternoon shift when the police were requested to assist medical and social care professionals execute a warrant under the Mental Health Act – to assess someone to see if they needed sectioning in a dedicated mental health facility. These warrants specifically require a constable to be present as the people being assessed can often be quite unpredictable.

Two of my team attended but the male refused to allow anyone entry to his flat and a bit of a stand-off followed. I was monitoring this on the radio from the office, but it wasn't anything too out the ordinary and I trusted that the officers there would be able to resolve it, especially with the partner agency professionals there too. After some negotiation they eventually got in, but when they did they were confronted by some kind of doomsday prepper's wet dream. The whole house was rigged up with CCTV cameras, there was a ham radio in a corner, background noise frequency recorders and numerous other conspiracy theory paranoia type devices.

Most concerning however was the handgun laying in plain view on the coffee table and jars full of screws and ball bearings dotted around the room. My officers quickly dived on the suspect, handcuffing him and updated via their radios about what they'd come across. If there was one thing guaranteed to get me travelling out to a job pretty pronto it was that update! When I arrived not only did I see those items, but the cops showed me some wires going across the floor connected up to large plastic panels hanging out the windows. There was also a large box on the back of the front door with a skull and crossbones sticker on it which was clearly wired into the mains. Car batteries were wired up to all sorts of things that we couldn't establish the nature of. Oh, and there was also some cannabis in the address... These all set some seriously major alarm bells ringing and I made the decision to arrest the male for the possession of cannabis and he could be assessed for his mental health prior to being dealt with in custody. It also meant that we could remove him from the flat and perform a more thorough search of the address and investigate and secure the gun and all the other equipment.

Firearms officers came and confirmed the gun and a second one that we'd found as being ball-bearing airsoft guns, and therefore legal to own in the home. They were equally as concerned as I was about the other items though. To top it all off, intelligence checks showed that a quantity of ammonium nitrate had been ordered to the address recently – a key component in bomb making. All this combined meant that I decided we needed to evacuate the remainder of the flats in the building and call out the Joint Services Explosive Ordinance Disposal Team – the bomb squad. I spent the next several hours on phone calls to CID, Special Branch, the Control Room Chief Inspector and my own Inspector, as well as liaising with the bomb disposal team leader. I volunteered to remain at the scene myself and do the searches with the bomb squad, directing all the other officers to staff the external cordons. Never ask other to do something you wouldn't do yourself! I never told my wife about that when informing her why I was several hours late off work that night. I thought it best she didn't know these kind of things...

The bomb squad arrived and I took their team leader to see the flat. He quickly ascertained that the devices hanging out the windows were solar panels that were providing power to various TV's and radio equipment etc. The box on the back of the door with the skull and crossbones on he was less sure about. They took an x-ray of it and thankfully found it to be some kind of emergency door bolting device and declared it was safe.

The house was crammed full of clutter and by this time it was getting late and dark so there wasn't enough staff or light to conduct a proper in-depth search of the address. Given the intelligence around the purchasing of the bomb making chemical and the jars full of screws I didn't want to stand the scene down and therefore arranged for a comprehensive search of the address by a specialist team in the morning. The bomb squad left but said that they'd return if anything else suspicious was found.

I came in to work the following afternoon to be informed that in the morning the specialist search team had found what were assessed by the bomb squad team to be two viable pipe bombs hidden at the address. The male was charged and remanded into custody after being deemed fit to be dealt with criminally following his mental health assessment. Even though he may have been mentally well enough to be dealt with, it was still clear that he had significant additional issues, that hopefully could be seen to whilst he was in custody. This was a classic example of the fact that you never know what is going on behind closed doors in the privacy of people's homes. Your neighbours could regularly be suffering from or inflicting domestic abuse; have the house transformed into a cannabis growing factory; or even making bombs, and quite often you'll be none the wiser.

***

Being the Sergeant often meant that I would patrol on my own on night shifts if there was an odd number of officers on duty. It also meant that I was sent to fewer incidents by the control room dispatchers in case I was needed to attend a job that required a supervisor. This meant that I spent more time on patrol driving around and as a result could see more things as I wouldn't be stuck at incidents. Some of these were very sad, especially where animals were involved. I came across several dead cats that had obviously been run over; the most heart-breaking occasion being when I found one which had a collar on with an address a few doors away from where it had been hit. I knocked on the door to notify the owners. It was early evening time and as the homeowner opened the door I could see two young children behind them in their pyjamas ready for bed. I explained as quietly as possible to the adult about the cat and took them to see it, where they confirmed it was their beloved family pet. They went back to the house and told the children who came to see it and both promptly broke down in tears.

Also notably upsetting was the occasion on a night shift where it had been raining and I came across a family of ducks lying in the middle of the road. They had presumably mistaken the dark wet tarmac for a pond. The male duck and a gaggle of ducklings had been hit by a vehicle, leaving the female duck stood at the side of the road, the only survivor. It was mournfully quacking at the other ducks, as if to hurry them up and get them to follow it seemingly not understanding that they were all dead.

Animals also sometimes provided some comic relief though. Early in my time as Sergeant I'd taken one of the more experienced team members out on patrol one night to get to know him. We were patrolling the area when all of a sudden a rather large white rabbit hopped into the road in front of us, causing me to slam the brakes on. It was definitely not a wild rabbit and had obviously escaped from a garden nearby. Either that or we were about to embark on a fantastical adventure with the Cheshire Cat... Doing our good deed for the community we decided to try and capture it and return it to wherever it had escaped from. We managed to corner it on a driveway and I grabbed it, wrapping my arms around its initially very actively kicking legs. A quick search around the immediate area resulted in us locating an empty rabbit hutch in a nearby garden; the only issue being it was the other side of a six-foot-tall locked gate. Knocking on the door of the address got no response – fairly understandably given that it was about 3am. My lanky colleague managed to get into the garden and I passed the rabbit over to him to put it back in its hutch. As is typical of so many things the police do, the owners would never know about the good deed done to them by the police that night.

It was only a few minutes later that the chronic itching of my arms reminded me about my bad animal hair allergy! I was driving the police car but had to switch with my colleague as my reaction got worse and worse. My arms and face itched terribly and my eyes puffed up to the point that I could barely see. By this time we'd been dispatched to a blue-light job for reports of a car having driven into a river. It turned out to only be a small water-filled ditch, but the driver was very drunk and we had to arrest him. It took about half an hour to deal with at the scene, throughout which my eyes were streaming and I could barely see! We transported the drunk driver to custody, where the general response from all the staff down there when they saw me went along the lines of "bloody hell! What's happened to you?" I saw myself in a mirror and looked like Will Smith in the famous scene from the film *Hitch*. The custody nurse was very helpful and gave me several anti-histamine tablets which along with a good face wash got the issue back under control. It took quite a while (and some cakes...) to live that down with the shift though.

***

I featured on social media again on my time as a Sergeant, but this occasion was entirely outside of my control. It was a rare afternoon where I'd completed all my admin and had actually managed to get out on patrol. Old habits died hard and I had the

ANPR system on in the car, when an alert made me aware of a vehicle that had recently been seen in suspicious circumstances in another city. I wasn't far from where it had been seen and I managed to get behind it, stopping it on one of the main roads into the city.

I went to speak to the driver and immediately noticed that the passenger didn't just have a mobile phone filming me, but an actual hand-held camcorder. I was used to being recorded on mobile phones during my time on the Knife Crime Team but on a professional video camera was a first. The driver initially seemed semi-reasonable but it was soon apparent that it was a veiled politeness masking actual contempt. It didn't take long for him to start claiming police harassment and asking why I hadn't got better things to be doing. He then told me he was a politician and was in Nottingham to conduct "anti-grooming patrols", explaining that there had been instances of young girls being groomed by gangs in the city. Sexual exploitation of young girls certainly occurs in Nottingham, as with every other town and city in the country and Nottinghamshire Police take it extremely seriously, but I had never heard of a civilian undertaking "anti-grooming patrols". I didn't really ask too many questions about it as what he wanted to do was largely his own business. I just needed his details and that of any of the other occupants, in relation to the marker on his car.

When I'd stopped him, another car had stopped behind him as well. I'd initially thought had been another motorist thinking I was signalling them to stop, but actually they were in convoy with the first car. I went to speak to that driver and noticed stacks of leaflets piled up on the rear seat. I explained to this driver and to the by now quite angry and sarcastic male driver of the original car that if they intended to distribute leaflets in Nottingham they needed a permit from the council. This advice was met with derision and I was told contemptuously that they didn't need a permit and that they could give out political leaflets if they chose to. They weren't interested in what I had to say, but continued to film and try and make out that they had outsmarted me and tried to verbally trip me up – unsuccessfully. After ascertaining the details of the people present I informed them they were free to go, but as is so often the case in these situations they wanted the last word and instead told me to go. I wasn't going to mess around and had done what I needed to, so happily got back in my car and drove off.

A few hours later the force started getting reports of anti-Muslim leaflets linked to the *Britain First* political party being left on cars in the Forest Recreation Ground car park in Forest Fields – quite a densely Muslim area of the city. The description of these leaflets made it obvious that they were the same ones that had been in the back of the car that I'd stopped a short time before. A council community warden went and collected all the leaflets off the car windscreens before they caused offence to anyone in the local area and brought them back to the police station. I saw the leaflets and on them was a picture of the male I had stopped. Apparently he was Paul Golding the leader of *Britain First*, a far-right political party. I'd had no idea who he was at the time I stopped him but had got the impression he was something to do with the far-right from his "anti-grooming patrols" comment. I told the council warden that I'd seen the leaflets in the cars I'd stopped and that I'd explained about needing a permit to give them out. Maybe they had listened to me after all and had decided to fly-post the leaflets under car windscreens instead. Unfortunately this meant several had blown off and created litter, so the council warden told me that if I could provide him a witness statement, he could prosecute Golding and the driver of the other vehicle for the heinous crime of littering!

A few days later I started getting messages off colleagues and friends with a link to a YouTube video. The female passenger of

Golding's car who had filmed the interaction had uploaded it to the video sharing site. The video had carefully edited out several parts where I'd explained to Golding the reasons why I had stopped him and where he had been particularly rude to me. All the messages I got from friends and colleagues all said how arrogant Golding came across and how well I had dealt with the situation, keeping my patience. This was a skill I had built up whilst on Knife Crime and often dealing with people thrusting camera phones in my face and trying to trip me up or supposedly outsmart me. The video has since been removed from YouTube along with most other *Britain First* content. Days after I stopped him, Golding was charged with terrorism offences, after he'd previously had his mobile confiscated by police and he'd refused to disclose the PIN.

This wasn't the only time I'd dealt with a politician, after a previous incident where I had had an interaction with a foreign diplomat. Police had been called to a local meeting venue for reports of a large crowd gathering outside and being threatening. When we got there, there was indeed a large crowd of a couple dozen people, some with sticks in their hands and all trying to get into the meeting venue with a few more larger built individuals trying to prevent them. There were only a couple of cops there – representing every officer that was available at the time. I managed to speak to someone who appeared to be the ringleader of one of the groups. He explained that there was a meeting of the Eritrean community taking place in the building, and the ambassador was due to arrive imminently to address them. He asked if I knew much about the situation in Eritrea, which I didn't, so he explained that there was essentially a civil war taking place there with pro- and anti-government factions fighting each another. The group inside the meeting venue were from the pro-government side and the protestors outside trying to disrupt the meeting were from the anti-government faction.

There were only a few of us police officers present, so our requests for the protesting group to disperse fell largely on deaf ears. We urgently requested additional officers to join us and a couple of neighbourhood officers and PCSO's arrived along with a couple of cops from neighbouring areas, but we were still heavily outnumbered and it was clear that the disruptive element could turn violent at any time – from both sides of the political divide. As a police officer you can get a sense of unease in certain situations even if there are no physical indicators of immediate violence. It's something that officers working Friday and Saturday nights in the city occasionally felt, and it was something that those of us present at that time were all feeling too. Things could go wrong at any minute.

The Eritrean Ambassador arrived then and attempted to drive straight up to the door of the meeting place to get in. His car was literally mobbed by the protest group trying to attack it. What few of us officers there were piled in and managed to get the protestors back and I told the car's driver to park on a nearby street out of sight where I went and spoke with the ambassador's bodyguards. They were adamant that as the police we had a duty to facilitate the lawful addressing by the ambassador of his people and it was our responsibility to guarantee his safety. I tried to explain that we would do our best endeavours to achieve that, but highlighted the very limited number of officers I had present. Their reply was simply "get more officers here then". My attempt at explaining the 'Policing by Consent' model of British policing, the right to protest, and the limited numbers of staff on at any time, especially in a provincial rural police force, fell largely on deaf ears. It appeared that policing in Eritrea was undertaken somewhat differently.

Luckily for me it was a Saturday and there was a home football game on, which had not long finished. I was able to request a couple of van loads of officers join me. With these extra officers, as well as the fact that by now an hour or two had passed, we did manage to facilitate the ambassador entering the building, by a side door. We even made a show of having his car try and get in again and then driving off, to make it look as if he had left. This ruse worked and almost all the protestors dispersed. A few of us remained in the area until the diplomat had given his address and actually left. I never saw him with any Ferrero Rocher though, which shattered my preconceptions about ambassadors. He certainly didn't spoil us with anything, thanks or otherwise.

***

Facilitating the visit of a foreign ambassador wasn't even the most surreal experience of my supervisory period. That was to come from an interaction with a five-year-old child of all things.

We'd had a call from the air ambulance crew that a group of Travellers were attempting to break onto the field where their helicopter landed. The crew had been forced to get back into the helicopter and take off rapidly otherwise the presence of people and vehicles on their site would have meant they couldn't lift off. Of course this possible negating of the air ambulance helicopter landing site prompted a rapid response from the police and several of my team attended. I was in the station so I hastily printed off copies of a notice that police are permitted to use to instruct Travellers to move on if they are on a site of particular disruption. I'd successfully used it before when some had pitched up on a school playing field and felt that the air ambulance landing site probably also qualified. I then hastily joined my team, but by this time I think the Travellers had realised their error and instead moved to a field opposite that was owned by the council.

This new field meant that they were no longer causing any significant issues and as such I quickly made the decision that I would not be requiring them to move on. I did however check their number plates against the Police National Computer, discovering that one of the vehicles had been caught speeding recently and the speed camera team needed the driver's details. I went to speak to the female occupant of the caravan next to the vehicle. I politely tried to explain why I needed to talk to her, but she was instantly hostile and began shouting at me in a rapid broad Irish accent. The fact that her young children were stood right next to her didn't stop her from calling me all the profanities under the sun. I tried reasoning with her but she just kept swearing at me and refused to give me the details I was asking for.

She then turned to her son, who cannot have been older than five, and said to him "make him go away, make the officer go away", at which point the five year old began attacking me with a horse-whip that he had in his hand! He smacked me four or five times with the whip, which although he was not able to swing it hard, is designed to sting even with low force used. There was clearly going to be no negotiating in this situation, and arresting the woman with four or five young children with her was also not a realistic option. At this point weighing up the pros and cons I decided that discretion was the better part of valour and walked away. The only way I would be getting the information I needed out of her would have been to arrest her, taking her away from her young children, and also risk provoking the other Travellers on the site. Police officers are expected to be proportionate in their actions which arresting her clearly wasn't going to be. Sadly this woman seemed to know that and wasn't going to answer my questions.

It's not an uncommon tactic in *certain* sections of the Traveller community (not all) for the men to be off-site all day to avoid any potential police interaction and only return at night when the police are less likely to come looking for them. It also means that the police are less likely to arrest the women on site as it then leaves the children uncared for. Unfortunately on this occasion the tactic had worked, and sometimes there is no other way around this. It just meant that the vehicle would need to be stopped whilst driving instead.

***

Some of the most difficult situations that arise for a supervisor are when multiple things go wrong at once. One of the busiest days that I had was on the day of 'Storm Ciara' in February 2020.

The main Clifton Bridge out of the city had been closed only a day or two before due to dangerous structural defects. This had caused the whole south side of the city to grind to a halt at rush hours and had seen Nottingham become the most congested city in the world for a day! On this particular day there were really high winds and we'd spent most the shift responding to reports of temporary road signs blowing over into the road. We then received reports that a tower crane in the city centre was swaying dangerously in the wind, and that building materials from a separate large construction project in the city were also flying out of upper storeys and landing on the roads below. I was covering the city centre that day as well as my normal area, because the Sergeant there was off.

We were forced to close several roads in the area around where the large sheets of plasterboard were landing. There were nowhere near enough officers to close all the roads we needed to, so a request was made to the council to assist with road closure signs. To their massive credit instead of sending out a team with some cones and signs that in all likelihood would have blown over, the council sent out bin lorries that parked completely across the main roads to block them off! Partnership working and outside-the-box thinking at its finest. We managed to get hold of an on-call contractor for the site who came out with a team and secured all the materials within an hour of the first reports, which was quite an accomplishment. The director of the company for the tower crane was also able to confirm from video footage sent to him that the crane was within its normal acceptable sway limits.

It wasn't long however before more issues occurred to compound the already stressful day. A serious car crash on Alfreton Road at Bobbersmill Bridge, one of the key routes out the city to the M1, meant I had to close the road for about 20 minutes whilst the fire brigade worked to free one of the occupants of the vehicles. Simultaneously a tree fell across the road on Derby Road between QMC and Priory islands completely blocking that road. This is another key trunk route out the city heading to Derby and also the M1. The closure of both these roads, as well as the Clifton Bridge meant that three of the key arterial routes out of the city and to the M1 were closed at the same time. Luckily the Alfreton Road collision was resolved promptly before rush hour and the on-call emergency tree surgeons managed to get to Derby Road fairly quickly and re-open that too. It was quite literally the perfect storm, but thankfully some swift actions by police, partner agencies and private businesses stopped it from becoming a nightmare.

Trees falling across Derby Road between QMC and Priory Islands is not an uncommon occurrence and seems to happen once every few years. The worst I ever knew happened in around 2014 when a massive old oak tree on the boundary of Wollaton Park toppled over following days of torrential rain. The rain had meant that everyone was driving to work (instead of cycling or public transport) and the tree fell over at about 3pm, just in time for the afternoon school run. It was sheer good luck that no-one was injured by the collapse, but the closure of the road at this time caused gridlock, especially as the alternative route along University Boulevard had lane closures due to the tram lines being built. The entire city ground to a halt, which was only exacerbated by rush hour arriving. The council tree surgeons who were needed to clear the tree were already dealing with another urgent job in another part of the city that they couldn't leave part way through. They then got stuck in all the stationary traffic, unable to get to the site for hours.

It was a very wet and miserable few hours for me stood on a road closure at QMC Island. The worst part of duties like this is the ignorance often displayed by a small section of society. Despite police cars with lights on blocking the entrance to the road and a police officer stood waving traffic past, an all-too high number of people insist on asking:

"Excuse me, is this road closed?"

"Yes, I'm afraid it is."

"Why?"

"There's a large tree blocking the road completely"

"The whole road? Can't I get round it?"

"No, otherwise we'd have left a part open"

"But I only live just the other end of the road"

"Well unfortunately you need to go round"

"OK, so which way do I go?"

"Well, if you live nearby you'll know where you're going"

"But what way should I go?"

"Whatever way you want. Please keep moving."

Imagine this conversation punctuated by the sound of numerous car horns from the irate drivers behind, whilst I'm stood soaked through to the bone in torrential rain, and repeated time and again. Why some people are unable to use their initiative in situations like these is always beyond me. Some people also seem to feel entitled and not subject to the rules because they have been inconvenienced. It's not unheard of for people to drive around police cars and cones clearly parked blocking roads. I've had it happened to me a few times. They always get a ticket when they end up having to come back as they can't get past whatever was causing the road closure in the first place. Others either shout at or abuse the officer stood on the road closure, blaming them for that fact that they can't drive the route that they want to. They'll often also criticise the police for not putting up diversion signs. There seems to be no consideration that creating a diversion isn't something the police do; it isn't an immediate priority for the police or any other agency when dealing with a major incident; and the council or highways workers who will create the diversion are stuck in all the same traffic tailbacks as everyone else. I've found myself in similar situations in strange cities where the route I need was blocked by police closing the road, but I've always managed to find an alternative way without needing to berate or even speak to the officers on the road closure.

***

I saw out my career under the period of the Covid-19 Coronavirus pandemic. This was by far the strangest period of my service, as well as everyone's lives. Full lock-down meant that streets were largely deserted as people were instructed to stay indoors. As the police we were expected to enforce new legislation that had been hurried through parliament and was unknown in terms of how it would actually be implemented. A series of escalating monetary fines was introduced, £60 for a first-time offence, rising up to in excess of £1000 for repeat offenders. By-and-large the vast majority of people adhered to the lockdown rules – people didn't want to jeopardise their health and wellbeing, or that of their friends and family. At the beginning the fear was certainly very real as daily death tolls were published and the news had 24/7 rolling coverage of the opening of 'Nightingale Hospitals', and the Prime Minister addressed the nation every night whilst the public clapped for the NHS and all 'Key Workers' every Thursday evening at 19:00. As with any situation though, there are always those who either don't care or feel that they are above certain requirements and choose to flout them.

The introduction of the full lockdown period, with only essential travel and all shops and schools closed, saw a massive reduction in demand for the police across the country. There was an almost complete hiatus on all acquisitive crime (shops were shut, there was no-one out to rob and everyone was in their homes meaning they couldn't be burgled). Reports of domestic abuse plummeted *initially*, violence plummeted (no alcohol-fuelled drunken fights) and calls to anti-social behaviour ceased as well, with no-one being out their house loitering on street corners or having house parties etc. This meant that on-going investigations were completed hastily and there was very little in terms of current incidents requiring a police response.

The first few weeks were a real voyage into uncharted waters, as somewhat unbelievably it took the control room several weeks before someone in a position of authority felt that we could even *ask* every caller if they had any Covid symptoms! Prior to that there were concerns around breaching people's privacy – never mind about the health of officers that would be attending or their families. Obviously many of the incidents we would be required to attend would need us to go into people's houses, possibly even actively fighting with people who may well have the illness. That's not even considering those who would seek to intentionally cough or spit at police officers to cause them harm. There was understandably genuine concern from the team about attending incidents where people had symptoms and it didn't take long for us to resign ourselves to the fact that it was a case of 'when' not 'if' we caught the virus.

It wasn't long before the first instances of people intentionally coughing at police or other emergency service workers started. Thankfully the local judiciary were rightfully harsh on those guilty of this offence. The courts were closed but magistrates would hear remand cases by video link. 'Coughers' and 'spitters' were automatic remands and if they went before District Judge Pyle they were very likely to get an immediate six months imprisonment for their actions. These kinds of sentences were repeated nationally and the word soon got out, meaning many of those who may have considered such a course of action were suitably deterred. This was the same deterrent approach to sentencing that had been taken with the 2011 rioters and it works. It should be the norm. I firmly believe that currently we are too soft on those who commit serious crimes or crimes of choice (rather than largely forced by circumstance).

We continued about our daily business, answering calls to emergencies but also patrolling, reminding people that they should be in their homes unless exercising. It was a very difficult period because there was little clear guidance from the government about what was and what wasn't exercise and nationally some officers were criticised for being over-zealous (such as using drones to highlight walkers in Derbyshire) and others for not doing enough. As with all policing, it was a fine balance to walk where you can't please everyone and you're damned if you do and damned if you don't. Of course there were always those who were clearly breaking the rules. There was a ban on meeting up with anyone from another household so any group of three or four people who on initial glance didn't appear to live together meant that they would be stopped.

My pro-activity didn't stop just because there weren't the usual baddies or cars on the road, and the lack of on-going reviews and other live demand meant that I could actually get out on patrol as the Sergeant on a fairly regular basis. It was only a few days into the lockdown when I stopped a group of four young males walking together and after initially speaking to them it was clear that they were not of the same household. As the rules were fairly new we were still following guidance on 'Engage, Explain and Encourage' (to comply with the rules) rather than 'Enforcement'. The fixed penalty ticket procedure had not even been introduced at this stage. I took the details of the males and filmed it on my body worn video so that

I had their faces on film, told them all to go their separate ways and thought nothing more of it.

It was the very next day whilst out and about that I saw several of the same group, together again. Clearly this was now a wilful ignoring of the rules that were in place for everyone's safety. Not only were they out the house (albeit they could have been taking their daily exercise) but they were meeting up with people from other households and just happily walking next to each other laughing and joking. I went to stop the group again – bearing in mind that at this stage guidance around face masks was that we didn't need them outdoors, so every interaction was potentially placing ourselves in harm's way. They immediately split up and started walking off in different directions as soon as I pulled the police car up next to them. I went to stop the one who I definitely knew was one of the same ones from the previous day. Initially he clearly ignored my requests to stop until I took hold of his shoulder and escorted him to the side of the pavement where I started asking for his details – name, address and date of birth. These were completely different to the ones he'd given me the previous day. Unluckily for him I don't think he recognised me (all police officers look the same in their uniform to most people) but I was able to show him where he had written his false name in my notebook the previous day. It suddenly dawned on him that he'd been caught out and he pivoted on the spot and ran off down the road.

It seems to me from my experience that a certain percentage of law-breakers must lead lazy lives with very little exercise, and this male was no exception. He managed about 50 yards before he was clearly out of breath and gave up the chase. I caught up with him and arrested him for obstructing a police officer. I also arrested him for failing to abide by the rule of not meeting up with anyone from outside your own household, under the Coronavirus Regulations. I explained that I had no other choice than to arrest him as he had not told me his name or his address. He then began to give me yet another set of details and pleading with me not to arrest him. Anyone who starts pleading to the extent that this male did usually has something to hide and often means they're wanted for something else and don't want their fingerprints taken in custody. I explained that as he'd given me several different names I had little choice but to arrest him unless he could confirm his name some other way, such as with a passport or similar. He said he would tell me his address and that his ID documents would be in there. As this address was on the route to the custody suite anyway, I agreed to take him there.

We pulled up outside the address he claimed to live at and a colleague came to watch him whilst I went to speak to the occupants of the house to get his documents. The chap I'd detained started shouting loudly in another language from the back of my police car to the male in the house, which always sets alarm bells ringing. Why did he need to frantically shout something to the occupant before I even had chance to speak? The person in the address clearly wasn't bothered though, as they denied that the lad I'd arrested lived there. There was now no other option but to go to custody.

When I got to custody I explained the circumstances of the arrest and what I'd arrested the male for. I then had a disagreement with the custody Sergeant who was arguing that the new Covid offences were not arrestable, only able to be issued a ticket for. I explained that as I could not establish the male's name and address I could not ticket him and therefore had no option but to arrest him. The custody Sergeant eventually relented and booked the male into custody, but made me wait with him until one of my team had been to yet *another* address the chap had given. Luckily this time his passport was there. My arrested suspect was charged with obstructing a police officer and bailed pending what decision the Home Office were making with regards to disposal of Covid offences. A few days later the formal guidance came out and the male was issued with a ticket.

Clearly not deterred by the threat of the fine that he would receive at some point in the future, I stopped the same male a further two occasions breaching the rules, and two separate colleagues also stopped him! He was the first person in the county to be arrested for breaching the Coronavirus Regulations, and also likely the first to receive five tickets taking him to the maximum £1000 fine. The entire legislation had been contentious from when it was introduced, but, during this first lockdown at least, the guidance to everyone could not have been clearer. I didn't feel sorry for this chap, who by his actions was consistently placing not only himself but anyone he came into contact with at significant risk. And it's worth repeating that at this early stage of the pandemic, no-one knew how harmful or transmissible the disease was.

I handed out a couple of tickets to other people later in the lockdown too, including a pair who were having an afternoon drinking session on the Forest Recreation Ground. I found them surrounded by empty cans of alcohol, but they still tried claiming that they were on their daily exercise and had just stopped for a picnic. The only exercise they were getting was their right arms from the ground to their mouths...

Nottingham has a large student demographic, with figures suggesting that the city's population increases by some 30,000 or more during the two universities' term times. We'd experienced the first wave of the Covid-19 crisis in the lockdown of March and April and the numbers had significantly dropped off to a stable level over the summer. Then in late September the government made the decision that it was safe for the students to return to face-to-face learning. I can to an extent understand the government's rationale behind this. The universities need funds from the students to continue vital research work and ensure they don't close; the students need to progress their learning which in probably a significant percentage of subjects can't be done effectively remotely; and people need to return to some semblance of a normal life – especially the students who had seen their A Levels and last school year disrupted so badly.

Unfortunately this created a perfect storm in the city, where 30,000 additional people boosted the population with no additional space. This demographic also had the university mentality, where they wanted to go out drinking and enjoying their new-found freedom having moved out from home. There was the additional issue that student halls of residence are fundamentally designed to cram as many people into as small of a space as possible. None of this was conducive to social distancing and preventing the spread of Covid-19 which had been done so effectively over the spring and summer. My experience of 'Freshers' Week', when the first group of students returned, demonstrated excellently why there was a subsequent huge spike in Covid-19 cases in the city during September and October. I went to countless student house parties – there were a dozen or more a night that we attended in the few days leading up to the first 'rule of six' being introduced, with the students trying to beat the deadline. Even after that I attended several more parties, including once that comprised of 200+ people taking over a whole block at a halls of residence. With the best will in the world, the six of us that were available on that shift could only collar a small handful of the participants. It was all we could do to chase the bulk of them away and then remain parked outside the halls in the marked police cars for an hour or so to ensure that they didn't return.

Almost certainly the large majority of the students were abiding by all the guidelines, avoiding unnecessary contact and maintaining social distancing. Unfortunately all it takes is one person from each flat in a student halls to attend a party or spend time with someone who did and that person would then give it to all the others of their flat through being forced to share kitchen and hallway space. This resulted in hundreds or even thousands of students contracting Covid-19 and having to isolate themselves in halls of residence that became quasi-prisons. Official statistics showed that 400 students caught the virus. I was told by someone who worked for Nottingham University that their pro-active (non-government reportable) in-house testing of all students revealed as many as ten times that number had it. Nottingham was placed into the highest level of restrictions in the weeks after this, along with most other big university cities.

***

It was during the Covid summer of 2020 that the Black Lives Matter movement also really took off too. This had largely stemmed from America and unequal rights there, but had spread to the UK with many of the ideas seemingly transplanted directly with little thought given to the vast differences on this side of the Atlantic. These campaign elements included accusations of excessive police brutality towards the BAME community, which may exist in America but which I have personally never witnessed in the UK. I'm not saying it doesn't exist, and there are occasionally well documented cases of it, but certainly to nowhere near the extent it appears to be in America. I have mentioned the oft-quoted statistic that those of BAME backgrounds are significantly more likely to be stopped and searched by the police than those of a white background. I've already shown how this is poor journalism or a gross simplification of statistics to make poor and ill-thought out political points. The truth behind the figures can be quite complicated to both explain and understand however and is not as headline-grabbing as "BAME people are eight times more likely to be searched". This, coupled with sensationalist media stories about routine stops of people who happen to be from a BAME background and claim that was the sole reason for their stop, whipped up some kind of anti-police frenzy and meant that the police became a key focus of the Black Lives Matter movement.

It was in this climate that demonstrations were organised by BLM to campaign for equality for their communities. The first of these was organised exceptionally well by several young people with no previous experience of organising protests. They'd arranged for guest speakers, complied with social distancing and arranged it to be on the Forest Recreation Ground, providing sufficient space for large numbers to attend. No trouble was anticipated and there were only a handful of PCSO's deployed to the area to provide a visible presence and protect the demonstrators from any counter protest. The rally went off very smoothly and was a huge credit to the organisers and attendees; but then unfortunately, as is so often the case with peaceful protests, it was hijacked by a small less well-behaved minority. This group of a hundred or so decided to march from the Forest Recreation Ground into town, along the middle of the main Mansfield Road. This created traffic chaos because no road closures had been put in place as no march had been planned. A police car even had to drive behind the group to prevent traffic hitting them and to enable their spontaneous demonstration. Bizarrely the officers in that car protecting were not subject to the anti-police sentiment of the small crowd they were escorting...

When the march reached the Old Market Square someone within the group sprayed graffiti over the Council House. This was selflessly cleaned off the following day by other members of the public who had been at the rally, disgusted at what others had done in their name and determined to not let the mindless hooliganism undermine their important message. After some chanting in the Market Square the group converged on Central Police Station. This was clearly a group who were anti-authority and the order went out for the police cars parked on the street outside to be moved immediately, lest they be targeted. Some of the protestors climbed onto the building's covered entrance whilst the remainder stood on the roundabout outside blocking the whole of Maid Marion Way. They then marched out of town down Alfreton Road, and the fear was that they were now coming to Radford Road police station.

Having not expected trouble due to the well-organised nature of the initial demonstration, there were no additional officers on duty and the request came over the radio for all day shift officers (which included my team and me) to remain on duty, and all who were riot trained to make their way to another police station, kit up and remain on standby there. This left myself and four of my team at Radford Road police station whilst the afternoon shift who had come on were all out at other normal incidents. We had CID officers coming to join us in the main parade room monitoring their radios too, fully expecting trouble, and as the protest march turned onto Gregory Boulevard we were sure they were now heading to Radford Road. Thankfully they returned to the Forest Rec and after another half an hour or so there, dispersed. There were genuine concerns that if the protestors had reached our station that they would have been more emboldened and worked-up and may have attacked the building. As the Sergeant I was having to portray a sense of calm to the team, especially to one new member of the shift who had only started the previous day! I had to explain to her that every day wasn't like this one...

***

It was during the pandemic, in the October of 2020 that I handed my notice in to Nottinghamshire Police. I had been approached and successfully applied for a position as a university lecturer, which enabled me to combine my passion for policing with my twin passion for academic study and research. It also allows me to spend more time with my young family and enjoy a better work / life balance. Perhaps policing is a young person's game, or perhaps I had just done too much of it and not got back as much as perhaps I thought I should. Certain previous incidents or attitudes had also spoilt my passion for the job leaving a slightly bitter taste, as well as having missed out on promotion on a few previous occasions.

Politics has come to have too much of an influence on policing and ever-increasing demands on police officers for ever decreasing pay meant it was no longer what I loved. Increased (excessive) requirements by the Crown Prosecution Service to massively increase the administrative burden on the police to prosecute criminals they catch; coupled with the simultaneous with which they would drop even the most nailed-on of cases really frustrated me. I joined to catch and prosecute baddies, not sit in an office completing endless paperwork and then having to wait a month for CPS to make a decision to prosecute them or not; only for them to send it back because I hadn't filled something out correctly in a box – or even not put "n/a" in a box to show that I had actively considered it – only to then have to send it back to them again and wait another month.

Senior officers would introduce policies that they *thought* might make things better. Too often this would only make things better for their team, and serve to increase the burden on others. These decisions would then simply often just be reversed by the subsequent person who took the post a year later. More and more burden was placed on front-line officers with fewer and fewer staff; ever increasing scrutiny with a real terms 20% pay cut during the length of my service. New recruits now start on barely above the minimum wage.

Shift work and lack of sleep also took a big toll on me. With two young children and a wife in a professional career, juggling life and childcare was always fraught. I had a sleep tracking watch that told me my average night's sleep was less than 6 hours – which included the more normal nights kip on rest days. Frequently I would only get 4 hours or so, which just wasn't sustainable. The irony was that the force recognised this and paid an external sleep expert to come ad deliver workshops. Emergency response officers – some of the only ones working full shift patterns – couldn't get the time off work to attend these due to minimum staffing issues, or would have had to come in on rest days without pay, losing more of their life to the job. The overwhelming majority of those who attended were not those working night shifts – and none of the solutions shared had any comment on how to balance rotating shifts and the demands of parenting. I know that this was a problem faced by police officers for generations, but up until perhaps my own generation, women were traditionally expected to primarily stay at home and raise children whilst men worked. In today's society where partners are rightly afforded equal opportunities, it places an unfair burden on the non-police partner to do far more than a fair share of childcare.

I have genuinely no idea how couples where both are police officers or on shifts cope. To those families, I salute you.

I was overwhelmed by the numbers of e-mails I got when I announced my departure, from people saying that they'd thought I would never leave the job and how passionate and keen I had been throughout my service. Some described me as one of the best police officers they'd encountered. Whether that's true or not I don't know, but I certainly always strived to give my all to 'The Job' and through being keen and always willing to go that bit further, I often found myself in the centre of some very good incidents, as has hopefully been shown through some of my anecdotes.

I really hope that you've enjoyed reading this and it has given you some flavour of policing in the 21st Century, and a flavour of Nottingham and what goes on here under the surface. I have consciously stuck to more interesting stories – the ones that you tell people about when they ask you to tell them some of the things that you do as a police officer, or the ones that you tell colleagues when you're joking or reminiscing about previous incidents. I haven't made any mention of the hundreds of domestic abuse calls that I have attended throughout my service, or the burglaries, robberies or all manner of other crimes that I've taken reports of over the years. This is not to belittle the victims of those offences, as they can be particularly awful offences to fall victim to, but unfortunately there is rarely much out of the norm of these incidents warranting me including them in this book.

I received several thank you cards during my service – not as many as I did complaints mind, which is probably either telling of society as a whole, or maybe just my nature – so I can only hope that I made some small difference to a few people's lives. I can also be fairly sure that there are at least a couple of people who are alive today through my actions who may otherwise not be. There are also victims who've received justice as a result of what I've done and been able to help them get some kind of closure. I know that my arrest figures number in the several hundreds, possibly over a thousand, and was certainly a very familiar face to all the staff in custody with how regularly I went down there. I also had some incredible life experiences, such as being able to drive legally at close to 130mph on occasion through the city. I've been trained to use an electrical incapacitation device (Taser) but thankfully never had to actually use it on anyone; incapacitant irritant spray; and a large metal telescopic baton. I've been in houses worth millions of pounds and houses where the occupants have next to nothing, and found that sometimes the people in the latter are far nicer than the people in the former. Sometimes of course, they are most definitely not. I have pioneered emerging police powers and abilities, and tried to maintain old ones. I've been fortunate to have learnt skills from some of the best cops I've known and hopefully tried to pass on some of my knowledge to others. I've made lifelong friends who I've laughed with, cried with, and on occasion laughed until I've cried with.

I still firmly believe that being a police officer is one of the most important and most rewarding jobs that someone can do, and one that is chronically undervalued and over-criticised by too many. In my new job lecturing student officers I give all of my passion, and some of my constructive criticism, to the next generation of police recruits, with the hope that they can go on and improve the service using the new evidence-based approach – trialling and testing new policies and procedures to actually see if they work and abandoning them if they don't.

Policing is a job like absolutely no other, and my utmost respect goes out to all those who continue to serve their communities without fear or favour, holding that thin blue line against the evils in the shadows. Especially those who join in spite of pressure from those close to them, or their communities in whatever form, against coming into the police. Also those who challenge outdated practice and policies by offering better ways of working – even when it significantly hampers your career, as I feel it did in my case. Thank you for standing up to be counted and looking to transform policing for the better by being the change.

To all those in blue, please keep at 'em and always remember the good jobs, even when you're at the worst. Policing is very much a family – you likely spend more time with your team than you do your nearest and dearest, so please look after each other, and ignore the negativity. Only those who have done the job can legitimately comment on your actions.

Don't let the bastards get you down.